Praise for *Reinventing Greatness*

"*Reinventing Greatness* is the best guide I have seen to help us lead ourselves and others through change. Practical and insightful, Shari brings her wealth of experience to show us how to move through life's challenges and changes with more ease and grace. If you are considering change in any part of your life or business, allow Shari and Lemon Squeezy to lead you along the trail. You won't be disappointed!"

—**Jayne Warrilow**, Founder of Coaches Business School, best-selling Author of *The 10 Day Coaches MBA*, www.CoachesBusinessSchool.com

"*Reinventing Greatness* is filled with insightful, actionable information that will help you create the reality you desire. This genuine, inspiring read will provide you with the tools you need for a successful reinvention so you can transform your life to be all you want it to be. If you only have time to read one book—this is definitely the book. It is extremely beneficial personally and professionally. Purchase your copy today—you'll be so glad you did."

—**Liz Johnson**, President & Principal Consultant, Mountain View Marketing, www.mountainviewmarketingllc.com

"In *Reinventing Greatness*, Shari has taken the incredibly complex process of personal reinvention and rendered it down to its essence. She draws her readers in with her engaging and humble storytelling about her own reinventions, including the one she has been on with Lemon Squeezy. This book is top on my list to give to my coaching clients who are in the midst of their own reinventions. If you are in the midst of reinvention, buy this book. It will be a warm and reassuring companion on your wonderful, wild, and sometimes bumpy reinvention ride. If you are not in the midst of reinvention, buy this book—sooner or later you will be."

—**Penny Potter**, PhD, Author, Educator, Coach,
Productive Interactions, www.productive-interactions.com

"I found great value in Shari's first book, *Take the Reins,* and had my leadership team do a book club on it. In *Reinventing Greatness*, the leadership journey continues. Shari's narrative regarding High-Impact Leadership outlines the three primary components that drive success. Her insights helped me develop one of the components and further strengthen the other two for higher impact. I encourage you to read Shari's book, and share it with leaders you know!"

— **Kathy Albarado**, CEO, Helios HR, www.helioshr.com

"Change is a fact of life for all of us, but few consciously navigate the process, and we suffer because of it. In her honest and insightful book, *Reinventing Greatness,* author Shari J. Goodwin shares the holistic process she's developed that consistently creates positive results for herself and her clients. Goodwin artfully guides the reader through heartfelt stories that illustrate easy-to-understand-and-implement tools to successfully—and mindfully—navigate any personal or professional life change. Everyone needs this book!"

—**Diane L. Haworth**, Coach/Speaker & Author of *How to Choose Love When You Just Want to Slap Somebody*, www.DianeHaworth.com

"I just read Shari's new book, *Reinventing Greatness*, and there are so many clients I want to share it with. She captures perfectly the inside-out work we must do to continually reinvent ourselves in this always changing world. This is a great read, and the horse tales add tons of drama to the story. I give this five stars!"

—**Holly Williams**, Founder of MAGUS Group Coaching, Co-Author of *Being Coached: Group and Team Coaching from the Inside*, www.magusgroup.com

"When facing fears in high-stakes change and uncertainty, *Reinventing Greatness* is a wisdom-packed antidote to claim opportunities, honor strengths, and do the difficult 'being' of leading. Prepare for Shari to elegantly guide and inspire you to tap into your power and resilience for the breakthroughs that await."

—**Cliff Kayser**, President and Founder, XPERIENCE, LLC, www.XperienceIT.com

"In her latest book, *Reinventing Greatness*, strategist Shari Goodwin's vulnerability and authenticity feel very real. She, who has reinvented her life many times, makes you feel like you too can overcome fear and adapt to your shifting environment in a way that instills confidence, clarity of direction, and renewed purpose. It's a handbook of inspiration and practical solutions that you will read over and over and use not only for yourself, but to encourage others as well."

—**Marianne Clyde**, Creator and Author of *Zentivity™: How to Eliminate Chaos, Stress and Discontent in Your Workplace*, and founder of the Be the Change Foundation, equipping women to be entrepreneurs, www.bethechangefoundation.us.

"Shari Goodwin's *Reinventing Greatness* is right on the mark. Who knew that as a sixtysomething lawyer-mother-wife I would be (and still am) reinventing myself? But I am and I do, largely with Shari's guidance. Over the years Shari has helped me discern what is in front of me, without judgment or swirl, so that I can step forward, which often includes an element of reinvention."

—**Katherine Armstrong**, Privacy Lawyer, Katherine.armstrong@dbr.com

"Reinventing Greatness: Leading Yourself and Others Through Change with Confidence and Trust is a book bursting with valuable and immediately actionable strategies for approaching and embracing the process of reinvention. Told through the wide eyes of a charming, curious, retired ex-racehorse, Lemon Squeezy, we see our own reactions to changing circumstances. Shari's personal stories vividly underscore the lessons she shares with humor and humility. As I cheered for Shari and Lemon Squeezy through their journeys, I realized I was also cheering for myself ... and for all the horses in the TRF herd and the humans whose lives are being reinvented, every day. If change is in your future (and I think that's true for all of us), read this book and share it."

—**Kimberly Weir**, Director, Thoroughbred Retirement Foundation (TRF) and TRF Second Chances Program, www.trfinc.org

REINVENTING GREATNESS

Leading Yourself & Others Through Change with Confidence & Trust

Shari J Goodwin

Shari J Goodwin

Jaeger2, LLC

P.O. Box 493

Marshall, VA 20116

www.jaeger2.com

Limits of Liability and Disclaimer of Warranty:

The authors and/or publisher shall not be liable for your misuse of this material. The contents are strictly for informational and educational purposes only.

Warning—Disclaimer:

The purpose of this book is to educate and entertain. The authors and/or publisher do not guarantee that anyone following these techniques, suggestions, tips, ideas, or strategies will become successful. The author and/or publisher shall have neither liability nor responsibility to anyone with respect to any loss or damage caused, or alleged to be caused, directly or indirectly by the information contained in this book. Further, readers should be aware that Internet websites listed in this work may have changed or disappeared between when this work was written and when it is read.

Printed and bound in the United States of America

ISBN: 978-0-9891844-2-7

Library of Congress Control Number: 2019904128

Acknowledgments

To my loyal and loving husband Jim, who believes in me more than I believe in myself and supports my passions, no matter how crazy.

To my parents Ray and Laura Jaeger, who raised me to be open to the infinite possibilities of the universe and for their steadfast love and support.

To my sister Jess, whose brilliant and creative brain keeps me from being too boring and for her generosity as my accountability partner on this book.

To my brother Saul, a perfect example of reinventing greatness and leading through change.

To my Uncle Jeff, who inspires my thinking with passion and joy.

To Lemon Squeezy. The universe brought us together, and I am forever grateful. Your kindness, wisdom, and gentle nature are gifts to us all.

To the rest of the herd—Cali, Frescoe, Lila, Noble, and Dixie in spirit—thank you for continuing to share your greatness and help with Lemon Squeezy. Our souls are connected for eternity.

To my friends who have been with me since the beginning of this adventure, Nancy David Dillon, Janet Dobbs, Sarah Atkins, Marianne Clyde, Diane Haworth, Bobbi McIntyre, Kara Dickey, Jeanette

Heath, Holly Williams, Katherine Armstrong, Yvonne Evers, Liz Johnson, and Kathy Albarado. I am so grateful for your support and guidance.

To all of my clients. Your courage, insight, depth, and willingness to forge a new path inspire me every day. You make the world a better place.

To my talented videographer and media guy Scott Harlan for filming in the dead of winter and for being a key part of my greatness team.

To my coaches and teachers Cliff Kayser, Penny Potter, and Jayne Warrilow for giving me confidence and guidance to launch Reinvention in the Round and for sharing their wisdom.

To my publishing partner Bethany Kelly, for her critical eye, support, and commitment to excellence. And to book coach Donna Kozik, whose programs help focus my writing.

To the natural world, my silent partner and biggest mentor.

Contents

Introduction

stepped off the elevator into the familiar corridor. Marble floors gleamed with polished wax. My boots clip-clopped like horses' hooves on pavement. I had walked this hallway hundreds of times in the past nine years. But today was different. I was different. I was a new business owner attending my first global conference on human potential. It felt great.

But as I neared the conference hall, my steps began to falter. Memories of past projects swirled in my head. My former environmental science clients worked across the courtyard. We ate lunch together in this same conference center. I felt drawn to go see them, to catch up and see friendly faces. My worlds were colliding. Doubt stopped me in my tracks. Everything was so familiar and so different. What was I doing here? Who was I now? For a moment, I wasn't sure. My mind raced. I took a deep breath, settled my nerves, and pressed on. I picked up my name badge and entered the conference hall into a sea of strangers. I was reinventing.

It wasn't the first time. Some people call me the "queen of reinvention." I've worked as an environmental scientist, a management consultant, an information technology staffing specialist, a waitress, a kennel manager, a horseback riding instructor, a business strategist, a leadership coach, a speaker, and an author. I spent 20 years in corporate positions and led winning proposals valued at up to $65 million. I ran a small start-up and grew it from 0 to $2.1 million in a year. I managed a team that helped prepare a technical litigation brief heard by the US Supreme Court. I balanced plates of pasta with sides of peas and beans, and spilled beer in a guy's lap. I've coached hundreds of leaders and entrepreneurs and witnessed their unique impact. And I've cleaned up a lot of horse manure.

Reinvention is both exciting and terrifying. You may change jobs, start a business, expand a business, or lead a team to a new ambitious goal. You may find yourself in a new spot as a result of an acquisition, reorganization, retirement, or life change. Or, perhaps the prestigious title you worked so hard for has lost its luster and you crave deeper meaning and impact. Reinvention is an opportunity to forge a new path, step into the unknown, and build something great. It's a leadership process of the deepest form and requires courage and commitment. Your way of doing things and your identity will be challenged. It may be bumpy before you land. But once you land, your world can be better than you ever thought possible. There is nothing better than living by your own design.

My first book, *Take the Reins! 7 Secrets to Inspired Leadership*, discussed the fundamentals of inspiring and motivating others to follow your lead. We partnered with my herd of horses as they shared their wisdom. In *Reinventing Greatness*, you'll meet the latest addition to my herd, Lemon Squeezy, a winning Thoroughbred ex-racehorse, as he reinvents into a new career. Lemon Squeezy's journey mirrors the many facets of change we all face during this process and parallels my own experience.

We'll highlight key learnings from our live workshops, a new program inspired by Lemon Squeezy called Reinvention in the Round. During these workshops, he and I worked together in front of an audience and explored what it takes to lead yourself and others through a reinvention. This format required me to step out in new ways as a leader, take chances, and be seen and heard more fully than ever before. There was no script. The content unfolded moment by moment. It was a little scary. At times I felt exposed, raw and vulnerable. The results were profound. Our sessions were videotaped and are available free on YouTube.[1]

Taking on this new horse and delivering Reinvention in the Round raised the bar for me. I barely knew Lemon Squeezy or how he would behave in these sessions, and the program format had never been tested. I hadn't worked with an ex-racehorse in years, and I'm not a professional horse trainer. One of my coaches said it was risky. It was. My credibility hung on the line for all to see. But this is the stuff of life. As leaders, we must be able to walk our talk and handle situations without preparation. To build something new, you must trust your instincts, take chances, and lead down an unknown path. You will make mistakes. There is no cookbook to follow.

In this book, we'll travel the reinvention journey together. We'll define the reinvention process and identify key steps you can take now to get started. We'll look at what it takes to be a safe space and inspire trust in the face of uncertainty. We'll review how to make great decisions and lead with impact. We'll learn strategies to break through resistance, overcome fear, and build resilience for long-term success. Along the way, I'll share my own experiences, examples from clients, and insights from Lemon Squeezy. Some of these stories are painful. A few times I almost gave up.

How you lead your life is your choice. There is no right way. But when you decide to honor your strengths and deepest desires, beautiful opportunities begin to emerge. Many of my clients are experiencing more financial abundance than they ever thought possible while enjoying their work, others have led their teams to new heights, including acquisitions and new contracts, and several have started new businesses to live by their own design. All are living more meaningful lives.

Here's the truth: At any moment, you have the power to reinvent.

Let's get started!

Chapter 1

What if I Said Yes?

Have you ever felt called to do something new? It begins as a vague urge deep in your subconscious. Slowly it begins to surface. At first you may ignore it. But it continues to knock, begging for the light. As it grabs for your attention and you dare to take a peek, the excuses begin to flow: "I'm too busy. It's not the right time. It's too risky. It seems silly. I can't afford it. It doesn't make any sense. I'm too old." So you stuff it. But it remains, lurking beneath the surface, waiting for another opportunity. Waiting for a "yes."

Saying yes to yourself and your goals takes courage. What if you say yes and fail? What if you succeed? Imagining either scenario may kindle your fear and paralyze your action. If you fail, you risk disappointing yourself and others. Your reputation, relationships, and income may suffer. You may fall into despair and be unable to find your way back. But if you succeed, your workload and commitments may consume you. Your free time may shrink. Others may see you differently and hold new expectations. Some may get jealous; a few may step away. You may feel pressured to maintain a certain image.

It's no wonder most people would rather play it safe. Taking a chance to live by your own design is risky. Leading through change is risky. But to reinvent, you must say yes to yourself and pursue what you want.

5

It can take some practice and finagling. You can create the reality you desire. But you must be willing to do whatever it takes.

I first said yes to myself after college graduation. In high school, I had visited Washington, DC, during cherry blossom season. The delicate pink and white flowers and fragrant scents mesmerized me and filled me with joy. The white marble monuments glinted in the sun and I could feel the passion, sacrifices, and commitments from our forefathers. I thought it was the most beautiful city in the world. Those men and women risked it all to create something great. I wanted to immerse myself in that energy. So I moved to Virginia, right across the Potomac River from Washington, DC. I had no job.

Virginia was known as horse country, and I was determined to own a horse and create the life I desired. I figured I could work as a waitress while I shopped my resume around for an entry-level corporate job. With dual degrees in zoology and English, I wasn't sure what firm would be interested, but shortly after moving to Virginia, I was hired by an environmental consulting firm. Lucky me. I met clients in Washington, DC. A plan was unfolding.

A few years later, I said yes to myself again when I bought Dixie, my first ex-racehorse. I only had $500, but that didn't stop me. Her price: $1,500. I reached into my pocket and handed the dealer $500 cash. I told him he would have the balance within three months. He agreed, and we shook hands. I had no idea how I would get the rest of the money or pay for her upkeep. But I found a waitressing job, worked nights after my day job, and cleaned stalls in exchange for board. It wasn't glamorous. Dixie was flighty and dumped me on the ground most weekends, but I loved her and she was mine. Sometimes saying yes to yourself results in pain. It was worth it.

Thus began a pattern that continued for much of my life. Each career reinvention moved me closer to horses as I worked to integrate my passions. Each business venture was a yes toward a life I imagined. Each failure was an opportunity to learn and grow and reposition myself. I jumped off and on the corporate track in between bursts of exuberant entrepreneurism.

Along the way, I bought more horses and a farm, and bred and showed horses. We reengineered our farm to include a custom barn and indoor arena, and I ran a boarding facility. Over the next several years, I made some big career moves: I resigned from corporate life, started a coaching firm, invented a leadership program, wrote a best seller, and gave lots of talks. I was finally working and living by my own design.

But a few years ago, I felt restless. Something was missing. I reflected and meditated and decided it was time to get a new horse. I never intended to buy another horse. Over the years, I'd owned ten horses. I thought my current herd of four would suffice for the rest of my riding life. But Cali, Frescoe, and Lila were aging, and they struggled with physical issues which forced retirement. Noble, the youngest at 15, had chronic back pain and lameness issues that annoyed us both. We spent thousands of dollars on chiropractic, osteopathy, anti-inflammatories, and various supplements, but couldn't get him consistently comfortable. Luckily all four horses are brilliant coaches in my equine-assisted learning program. Dixie had passed at a hearty old age of 31. I wasn't riding much and missed it.

Buying a new horse is a big deal. It's kind of like hiring a new business partner. You must be a good fit for each other, appreciate each other's strengths, and be able to compromise and trust. Buying a horse and hiring a new business partner are both expensive and time-consuming investments. Both are serious endeavors.

I haven't always held horse buying in such high regard. In fact, one time in my 20s I bought a horse on a Friday night out with a girlfriend. We were driving around and ended up at a horse auction. The next thing I knew, my hand shot up in the air, and "Crimson" was mine. That was a fluke not to be repeated. My husband almost divorced me. Crimson was a sweetheart, and Dixie loved her.

I hadn't purchased a horse for myself since I bought Cali in 2001. The rest of my herd had been either ex-racehorse rescues or the result of our breeding program, like Lila and Noble. Frescoe was purchased in-utero in 1998, before he was born. It was time to shop.

I developed a list of criteria for my new horse: quiet, sweet, confident on trails, solid at walk, trot, and canter, 12 years old or more, easy to load on a horse trailer, sound, and healthy. My goal was to find a good trail-riding partner. I no longer cared about competing or dealing with fresh-spirited youngsters. At 50 years old, I was done with young horse drama. Or so I thought.

Apparently the universe had other plans. I thought I was looking for a trail horse. I had no idea that saying yes this time would open a new frontier, change my life, shift my business, and profoundly impact many people. Here's what happened.

I browsed horse ads online and avoided any that said "flashy," "fancy," or "athletic." To me that was code for "drama." Instead, I looked at ads I never would have considered before: western-riding palominos, "child-safe" older horses, and smaller-sized horses around 15 hands. One "hand" is four inches. Most of my horses are 16+ hands with big strides and lofty movement. Frescoe almost tops 17 hands. I was ready for something different.

I drove to visit a 12-year-old former ranch horse described as "quiet and experienced." He was buckskin colored, gold with a brown mane and tail, and cute, but he looked at me with a suspicious eye. He seemed wary and distrustful. I decided not to ride him. Just as with people, you can tell a lot from looking at a horse's eye and expression. You get insights into its overall demeanor and way of seeing the world. A kind eye is critical to me. Although the horse had plenty of experience, I didn't feel we were a good match.

At the same location, a 9-year-old bay ex-racehorse was for sale. I definitely did not want that. But the farm owner thought I could be his perfect owner. The horse had a kind eye and seemed sweet, but had done nothing since retiring from the racetrack. I would be starting all over. I have a special place in my heart for ex-racehorses. I learned to ride as a youth at a Thoroughbred racehorse breeding and training farm, my first horse Dixie was an ex-racehorse, and I worked with many ex-racehorses in my 20s and 30s. But I was older now, with scars from former injuries. Those ex-racehorses require a lot of work. He met none of my criteria except for "sweet." My common sense told me to pass, so I did. I had no interest in repeating past patterns with ex-racehorses. Oh, really?

Little did I know, but a tiny seed was planted. A bigger plan was unfolding. I was oblivious.

Almost one year later, I found myself staring at another middle-aged buckskin horse. He was a Morgan, a breed I'd never owned, also a former ranch horse and great on trails. He was quite stunning, with an expressive personality. He glanced at me with confidence and wisdom. But as soon as my seat settled into the saddle, my gut said no. He marched off at a bold brisk walk. I could feel him taking over with his own agenda and way of doing things. He ignored my polite requests to go slower and felt set in his ways, kind of like an old cowboy. After one lap around the ring, I hopped off. I'm sure he was great at his job, but I'm not sure "compromise" was part of his personality. You've probably met some people like this. I prepared to go home.

As I walked to my car, the owner mentioned that they also had a quiet ex-racehorse for sale. The horse was six and hadn't done much since retiring from the racetrack. No, I don't want an ex-racehorse, I heard myself saying as I flashed back to last year's buckskin and ex-racehorse visit. But I didn't want to be rude. I walked back into the barn. The bay horse peered out from behind his hay pile. His kind intelligent eye and gentle aura beckoned. I entered the stall. He was small for a racehorse, only 15.2 hands, but looked sturdy and strong with great feet. I stroked his nose. He closed his eyes and made a sweet face. I felt my heart skip a beat.

The trainer tacked him up and rode him for a couple of minutes. The horse seemed sensible. I hopped on. What was I doing? I hadn't ridden a horse that inexperienced in years. But no alarm bells rang in my brain, no fear. My mind was silent and peaceful. We walked and trotted around the ring for about three minutes. He didn't know much, but seemed very willing to try and do whatever I asked. I stopped. I didn't need to ride more. Riding can be trained. It was no longer about the riding. I was speechless, a very rare moment for me. A chord struck deep inside me. A "yes" begged for the light. Could I say yes to this? What if I did? I barely remember dismounting. I do remember staggering back to my car and saying something about "I'll call you."

I knew right then that this horse had a calling. I could hear it. I knew that together we could help many people, if I dared. I knew he could be a tremendous new dimension to my existing equine-assisted leadership program and potentially become a powerful riding partner. I also knew that it would require me to step out in public in a much bigger way than I ever had before. I knew that I'd have to move beyond any physical fears of training and riding a young inexperienced horse. I was freaking myself out. Where was this coming from? It felt like divine intervention.

As I hopped in my car and drove away, an entire new business program downloaded into my brain. This horse could help leaders navigate the reinvention process. As he reinvented into a new career, I could coach him through the process, just as I do with clients. We could demonstrate the process and explore what it takes to lead yourself and others through change. We could videotape sessions and make them available to all. I could write a book. But he didn't meet any of my riding criteria, and I didn't want an ex-racehorse. Ex-racehorses could be dangerous and require a massive amount of retraining. I was too old, beat up, and emotionally spent to take on another project. Or so I assumed. My mind spun.

I scheduled another ride to be "sure." It was one torturous week before I saw him again. I reflected on the buckskin horses. Neither was a fit for me, but each had drawn me to bay ex-racehorses. If those buckskins had not captured my attention, I never would have met this horse. How weird.

The second ride was similar to the first. I was sure. I scheduled a vet exam, although I knew I would take him home no matter what. What the heck? Where was my rational brain? It was being totally overridden (pardon the pun) by the call. I must say yes to this call. To appease my rational brain, I also had blood work and a Lyme disease test run to check his health. The winter holiday break caused a two-week delay before we received the results. But even if he had Lyme disease, I was going to take him. Normally I am rational and analytical. But this calling was bigger than rational and bigger than me. Universal energy or something was guiding this process. I was but a tool.

He passed the vet exam and his blood work was clean. On December 29, 2017, one of the coldest days of winter, I brought him home. His registered name was Lemon Kay. We decided to call him "Lemon Squeezy" after my husband reminded me that I always say, "easy peasy lemon squeezy." My coach thought the name was great. I thought it was ridiculous. But something about it was just perfect. It stuck.

In our first year together, Lemon Squeezy inspired the development of a series of workshops that I called Reinvention in the Round, the Reinventing Greatness Retreat, and numerous talks on reinvention to business professionals and leaders. I also wrote the first draft of this book. Many called his work "life-changing." Saying yes to this calling opened many new doors for me and others.

I'd love to say that our riding training went perfectly, but that would be dishonest. He's not the quiet, experienced, safe horse I set out to purchase. He's a fresh young athlete with opinions and fears. He's also sweet, intelligent, and willing to try almost anything. Our partnership is unfolding. I'm excited and optimistic about our future.

What can you say yes to? Open the door to what you most desire and take a peek inside. You don't have to make big changes. Dabble, experiment, and explore. Research something new, attend a training or conference, learn a new skill, go on a retreat, or talk with an industry expert. What's the tiniest "yes" you can agree to now? One small "yes" can pave the way to a reinvention.

In the next chapter, we'll review the reinvention process and what it takes to honor that "yes."

Chapter 2

The Reinvention Process and States of Transformation

Reinvention is a process of transformation. Merriam-Webster's dictionary defines it as "to remake or redo completely."[2] You may or may not "redo completely." Regardless, the reinvention process is the same and applies whether you're leading only yourself or a team through change. The process appears simple, but each step can trigger fear, spin you around, and stop you in your tracks. I've lived through this process many times, and even though I know it well, there are always new surprises. My optimistic side calls these "opportunities for growth." But must they be so painful? In this chapter, we'll take a close look at this process and explore what will move you forward and what may shut you down. Then we'll look at how these concepts showed up during my first session with Lemon Squeezy as he and I began his career reinvention.

The Reinvention Process

Reinvention is a process of transformation. It involves a change from one state of being to another. Success mentor and best-selling author David Neagle outlines five main steps for transformation, which can also be used to describe the reinvention process.[3]

1) Awareness

2) Decision

3) Change

4) Adapt

5) Grow

This is the path we all follow during any type of professional or personal reinvention or transformation, including starting, growing, and selling a business, career transitions, weight loss, and relationships, among others. Knowing where you are in the process may give you comfort and the clarity to continue to move forward.

It can be both exciting and scary to start down this path. Your commitment and ability to manage your fear dictate how far you will go. Although the steps appear sequential, reinvention is not linear. You may find yourself stuck at any point. For example, you may have awareness that you would like to make a change and make a decision to make the change, but never actually make the change. I've done that many times. Or, you make the change but never adapt to the new way of being or to the environment and end up sabotaging your results. Fear can hold you back.

Fear is a powerful and insidious force. It can permeate your mind and drive you to do things that sabotage your goal. You must be able to recognize it and reconcile it. To move forward, your "why" must be strong. If you are leading others through this process, you must also be aware of their fear triggers and help them feel safe. Let's dive a little deeper and explore how your energy impacts this journey.

States of Transformation

As you move through the reinvention process, you will flip back and forth between certain behaviors. At one moment you may feel confident and take lots of action, but the next day you may feel stuck. Why? At the most basic level, your behavior is driven by the competing energies of confidence and trust or fear. As your energy shifts back and forth, it influences your perspective and subsequent action or inaction.

To better understand these behaviors, I developed a simple pie chart. I call this chart "States of Transformation" to name the specific behaviors we experience as we navigate reinvention or any type of change.

STATES OF TRANSFORMATION

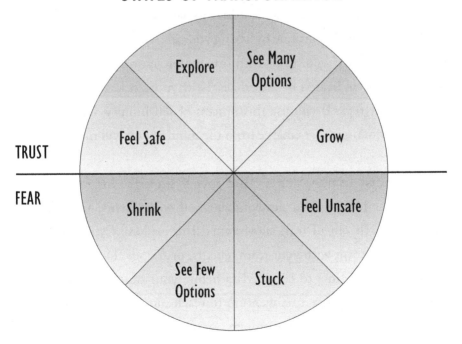

If you trust, you feel safe, begin to explore, see options, and eventually learn and grow. If you feel unsafe, the opposite may occur. You may feel stuck, see few options, and your world begins to shrink. But this is not a linear process. You may feel safe and begin to explore, and then fear hits. You feel unsafe and get stuck. We all move back and forth around and across this circle many times. If you are aware of where you are on this circle, it can give you clarity and confidence to move to a more desired spot. But how? Let's discuss.

How to Move from Fear to Confidence and Trust

We all have the power to shift from fear to trust and move forward toward our goals if we remember and direct this process. It's simple in concept, but it's definitely not easy.

If you happen to be on the fear side, ask yourself, "What would make me feel more safe?" Continue by asking yourself "What else?" and "What else?" until you feel your brain shift into a more rational thinking mode. This is usually indicated by an exhale. Now you can begin to relax and ponder next steps. If you use this process of self-inquiry and take baby steps on the actions that emerge from the inquiry, you will move yourself out of fear.

I've guided Lemon Squeezy and myself through this many times, and I use it for my own development and with clients. Once you've moved yourself out of fear, allow yourself to explore. Explore on your own or brainstorm with your team, clients, or friends. I call this "reconnaissance." It's a time to collect data before your next move. I encourage clients undergoing a reinvention to reach out to trusted colleagues, former co-workers, board members, or new contacts who are doing interesting things. Take trips, get involved in some pro bono work, or go on a one-day or half-day retreat. Suspend judgment and allow yourself to be fully present with the experience. The action doesn't have to "apply" directly to wherever you think you may be headed. Follow your curiosity and be open to gaining new insights and awareness.

When Lemon Squeezy feels safe, he begins to explore by sniffing the ground. He finds all kinds of interesting smells and often paws the ground in pursuit of the source. A horse never puts its head down unless it feels safe. With its head down, a horse may not see a threat. It is a very vulnerable position.

When you feel safe, it's easy to develop and implement a strategy to meet your goals. If you feel unsafe, the strategy you laid out when you felt safe may feel undoable and you may get stuck. Let's take a look at this process in action with Lemon Squeezy.

Reinvention in the Round with Lemon Squeezy —Our First Session

The reinvention process, fear, trust, and the states of transformation were on full display during our first session of Reinvention in the Round. It was February 3, 2018, and Lemon Squeezy had lived with us for about a month. His transition to our farm had been stressful. Freezing temperatures, blustery high winds, a new routine, and dominance challenges from the other horses caused him to be reactive and defensive. He threatened to kick me in his stall and bite me if I walked too close. He pinned back his ears and rushed at the other horses, teeth bared. He spooked at everything and blasted out of the ties we use while grooming. He was a handful, and I was a bit worried about this first workshop.

Since his arrival, I had only worked with him for about two weeks for a few minutes each day. I knew his difficult behavior was just a phase (or so I hoped!), and we were doing short non-riding exercises to build trust. I rode him one time, and I was out of control at the walk—I had no brakes, no steering, and absolutely no relationship with him. I hopped off. We needed to rebuild everything from the beginning. Even though I rode him twice before I bought him, he was a different horse in this environment, an unpredictable, fearful horse. I needed to start over to gain his trust.

We had about 30 people registered for the workshop, and I had no idea how he would react to all of the people and chairs, the multiple cameras that were taping the session, the microphone, the freezing cold weather (it was about 15 degrees F) and all of the other gear that was now in the arena. Prior to that day, he and I worked alone in that arena. I wasn't even sure if he would see me or listen to me in that setting. Perhaps this was a bit risky for me professionally, but I didn't care. Reinvention can be a messy process and it requires authenticity. It was worth the risk.

At the start of the session, he tried to hide behind me. A 1,000-pound horse trying to hide behind a human is a sight to see! At that moment, he wanted to disappear. He was fearful, stuck behind me, didn't see any options to do anything different, and looked almost as if he was trying to become invisible or shrink. His fear was palpable.

A few minutes later, he took a breath and began to trust. He felt safer and began to explore the arena. He left my side to explore other "options" in that space. He ambled about, sniffed the sand, and tasted the bars of the arena. You could see his confidence grow. At one point, he stood on the other side of the arena from me all alone. This was his choice. He could be wherever he desired. He showed all of the states of transformation within five minutes.

Later during that session, I rolled a large red exercise ball into the space with us. He spun around and shot away from the ball—a fear response. He snorted with suspicion and made grumbling sounds through his nose. This is how horses express uncertainty. He was back to feeling unsafe. He placed himself as far away from that ball as possible. But once he realized the ball was not attacking him, he began to gain confidence, to feel safe and explore the "new" environment with the ball. His confidence began to grow as he walked closer to the ball. Then I sat on the ball and bounced. That freaked him out. He galloped off, turned, and stared at me from across the arena. Fear was back. But a few minutes later, he inched closer and closer to me and the ball. He stopped a few feet away, stretched his neck and head out toward me, and blew softly into my face. His whiskers touched my cheek. He trusted me and felt safe. It was powerful to witness and brought tears to my eyes.

Lemon Squeezy demonstrated the entire reinvention process at least twice in 30 minutes. He showed how quickly you can decide to overcome fear, choose a new response, and adapt to a shifting environment. He also showed how fast you can lose confidence and shrink back. It reminded me that at any moment, there are infinite possibilities for your own experience. You can feel fear and then choose another feeling. You can choose to walk forward in trust. The more you experiment and expose yourself to these feelings, the better you will be able to use them to achieve your goal. Give yourself opportunities to practice trusting yourself and others. We'll talk more about trust and how to do this in the next chapter.

Chapter 3

Trust: Are You a Threat, Invisible, or a Safe Place?

In any relationship, trust is key. Trust helps you move forward. Reinvention requires deep trust.

During a reinvention, much is in flux, and uncertainty is high. Your organizational structure may shift, well-used protocols may no longer apply, client expectations may change, and timelines may be shorter. Sometimes you're asked to do more with less—fewer resources, less time, less experienced staff, less guidance. If you're reinventing on your own, you may not be clear on your own direction or the next step. *Terra firma* may feel elusive. It can be a volatile and exciting time.

Your perception of yourself, others, and even the environment influences how much you trust and the action you are willing to take. Perceptions can shift in an instant; trust can be lost in a moment. You must pay attention.

I thought I knew a lot about trust. My leadership model is based on trust, and almost every process flow diagram I create includes something about trust. In my first book, *Take the Reins! 7 Secrets to Inspired Leadership*, I wrote a chapter on how to trust and be attractive. I ran retreats called "Trusting Deeply" and led a "Trusting Deeply Mastermind." But I had a lot more to learn. The horses have been great teachers.

Over the years since my first book, I spent many hours observing what trust looks like and doesn't look like. I reviewed definitions of trust and began to explore its components. In this chapter, we'll look at the components of trust, how to evaluate it, and consider the three ways you may be perceived: as a threat, invisible, or as a safe place. For best results, be seen as a safe place. The horses will show us how.

What Does It Mean to Trust?

First, let's consider what it means to trust. The simplest dictionary definition of the verb form is "to place confidence in" (Merriam-Webster). But trust is dynamic and situational. You may trust someone under some circumstances but not under others. It is fickle and takes time to build. One incident can cause it to crash. Trust is also associative; if my friend trusts you, I am more likely to trust you. I was not satisfied with the dictionary definitions. So I dug deeper.

The Components of Trust: How Much Do You Trust?

There are many models and studies on trust. Some are quite complex, and new insights are always emerging. I prefer the simplicity of one model that describes trust as composed of three main dimensions: benevolence, competence, and predictability/reliability.[4] The three dimensions are defined below. Each is ranked on a scale of 1 to 5 (low to high) to determine the trust level.

1) Benevolence—I feel you have my best interests in mind.

2) Competence—I feel you have both the skills and motivation to do the job.

3) Predictability/Reliability—You do what you say you will do. Your behavior has been consistent enough over time that in high-stakes situations I know I can count on you.

The overall trust level is indicated by the lowest number ranking of the three dimensions.

I've adapted and used this approach to assess how much I trust myself and to gain clarity on my level of trust for other team members, supervisors, and clients. It's a very handy tool that can give powerful insights. I also used it to assess how much I trust Lemon Squeezy. Here's our trust assessment one month after he arrived:

Name: Lemon Squeezy
Assessor: Shari Goodwin
Date: Feb. 1, 2018

Trust Dimension	Comment	Rank (1–5)
Benevolence—Does he have my best interests at heart?	No, he feels threatened and only concerned about his own survival. He makes nasty faces.	0
Competence—Does he have the skills and motivation to do the job?	No, he doesn't know the job. He didn't know how to stop, turn, or what leg pressure means when I ride him. He is wild in the barn and broke out of cross-ties.	1
Predictability/Reliability—Does he behave in a consistent manner and do what I would expect?	No, he doesn't know what the expectations are and feels threatened in this new environment.	1

No wonder I didn't trust him! Now, let's look at me from his perspective.

Name: Shari Goodwin Assessor: Lemon Squeezy Date: Feb. 1, 2018		
Trust Dimension	Comment	Rank (1–5)
Benevolence—Does she have my best interests at heart?	Not sure, but she does feed me.	1
Competence—Does she have the skills and motivation to do the job?	I have no idea. I don't even know her.	0
Predictability/ Reliability—Does she behave in a consistent manner and do what I would expect?	She feeds me at the same time every day and keeps showing up, but I have no idea what to expect from her. All her training techniques are totally different from what I've been taught.	1

We had some work to do in all areas.

Consider this chart for your own use. Who are you assessing? What would another say about you? What would you say about yourself? What dimension needs work?

The Power of Perception: Are You a Threat, Invisible, or a Safe Place?

Working with Lemon Squeezy sparked new insights on the importance of perception and how we each see the world. Perception drives behavior. Most of the time, our perceptions are subconscious. We don't realize we're making them. In my observations, I watched Lemon Squeezy evaluate three things: his environment, others in his environment, and himself. Each was assessed as a threat, invisible—not physically seen or not important—or as a safe place, as shown in the chart below. His perceptions dictated his next move. Humans make these same assessments. We'll explore examples in a moment.

Awareness	Perception
Self	Threat
Others	Invisible
Environment	Safe Place

Looking through the lens of perception gives you insight into who you need to be and where you need to make shifts to best lead through change. Are you a threat? Invisible? A safe place?

To optimize trust, most of the time it's best to be perceived as a safe place. But sometimes being perceived as a threat or invisible has advantages, as long as you are intentional. For example, if you or someone you love is under attack, you may want to be perceived as a threat to the attacker. Other times, it may be beneficial to be a benign observer and maintain a low profile. In that case, you may prefer to be "invisible" and not noticed.

Here's the tricky part: How you think you are perceived and how others perceive you may differ. For example, one of my CEO clients was told by a colleague that she perceived her as a threat. The CEO was shocked. She considered herself a kind and caring leader. However, her colleague felt intimidated by the CEO's polished and formal presence. The colleague's courage and willingness to share her perception gave the CEO important feedback and an opportunity to shift her approach to make others more comfortable.

A shift in environment may also trigger a threat response. For example, this can happen when a company moves to a new space, or when someone moves into a new office. The new environment may be spacious and beautiful but lack the intimacy of the former space. This may cause people to behave differently while they adjust. Some may feel invisible. Others may feel great. Good leaders understand this and work to build a sense of unity and connection in the new space. This may include holding potluck lunches or other informal team gatherings. As a leader, it's important for you to be visible during the transition. This allows others to see you and feel safe. Do not hole up in your fancy new office!

A new office may also trigger new perceptions. A larger office reflects increased power and prestige. It may cause others to see you differently, especially if you have been promoted over your peers. You may see yourself differently. A peer who was passed over for a promotion may feel invisible.

Other situations may prompt a perception of being invisible. For example, I know many who have felt invisible during leadership team meetings and board discussions. This can occur when you offer a suggestion or comment that is not acknowledged. A few minutes later, someone else offers the same suggestion to great acclaim. It feels as if you said nothing, as if you were not heard, respected, or valued. Sometimes this is a power play, a deliberate effort by others to disregard your input. Sometimes someone else better communicated a similar suggestion. Regardless, this practice can silence important voices and drive out the best talent. Acknowledge others' input before adding your thoughts.

You may be invisible to yourself. In your attempt to work hard and serve others, your own needs may begin to suffer. If you ignore your needs and desires, your sense of self may disappear. You may also be a threat to yourself. Ignoring your own needs and self-care can be destructive both physically and mentally. Negative self-talk and thoughts create a toxic environment. When this happens, you don't trust yourself. It's a downward spiral which makes it difficult for you to lead yourself or others with confidence.

If you are a safe place for yourself and others, you create harmony and trust. You listen and share. You value your own input and that from others. By being a safe place, you create a safe environment for yourself and all around you. When we feel safe, we explore, see options, take chances, and grow.

Let's look at how this plays out with Lemon Squeezy and the horses.

Creating a Safe Space with Lemon Squeezy, Lila, and Frescoe

As Lemon Squeezy's leader and partner, I wanted to be a safe space for him. But when he first arrived, he was defensive and reactive. Everything was a threat, including me at times. When I walked toward his stall, he pinned his ears flat to his head, swished his tail, and snapped his teeth in aggression. He felt he had to defend "his turf" from me. That was not the trusting relationship I desired.

Other times I was invisible. Lemon Squeezy is terrified of cows and flies into a panic when he sees one. His heart races, his veins bulge, and he gallops off. If I'm leading him, I become invisible. A few times he's almost run me over. He sees his environment as a threat and doesn't see me at all.

He also does this when I'm riding. One window in our indoor riding arena faces the neighbor's cows. Although the cows are two fields away and across a stream, Lemon Squeezy wouldn't go anywhere near that end of the arena when he first arrived. Over time, he was able to stand and stare out the window. I would wait patiently while he assessed the situation. Many days he would spin away the moment a cow moved (which was all the time), but gradually he was able to stand still even when the cows moved. To most people watching, this looked like a huge waste of time and effort. But, it was a valuable investment in our relationship. He needed to know that I wasn't going to push him into danger. Over time, we were able to ride around the entire arena regardless of where the cows moved. Little victories, eh?

In contrast, my horse Lila is a trusted leader. She leads with confidence and love. Many times I've watched her guide a group of people she just met through a complicated maze of obstacles. She does this off-lead, like a mare guiding a foal. She has a collaborative style and seems to know exactly what is needed. If a client takes a new direction, she is quick to follow; she doesn't always have to lead. But if someone strays off course, she waits for them to come back, or moves in another direction until they follow her. She's also clear on what is safe and what is not safe.

One day we played with a plastic tarp for the first time. She snorted and jumped as I pulled it out from the corner of the arena. But she didn't run. She stayed right next to her client. Despite her own fear, she placed herself closest to the tarp and kept the client on her other side. Then she began to sniff the tarp. Each time the client made a move toward the tarp, Lila glanced at her as if to tell her to stay put. She would not let the client move toward the tarp until she had explored it herself.

After Lila deemed it safe, she stood guard close by and watched as the client walked closer to the tarp. I asked the client what she thought was going on. She said Lila was watching over her to be sure she was safe. She said it was a powerful role reversal. In her work and life, she is always the one responsible for keeping others safe; in this instance, Lila took that role. Lila transformed a perceived threat into a safe place.

Being in the presence of a leader you totally trust is rare. My horse Frescoe is one of those rare trusted leaders. His herd respects him and trusts his judgment. I respect him and trust his judgment. Once he ran a bear out of his field. He stuck his tail straight up in the air like a flag, snorted, arched his neck and charged toward it. The bear sped across the field and leaped over the fence just in time.

Another time, I was riding Frescoe during a lesson in our indoor arena. A freak storm blew in. 80+ mph winds battered the walls. The temperature dropped about 30 degrees. People shouted and scrambled to close doors and windows, grab coats and hunker down. Rain and sleet sheeted down in sideways torrents. Frescoe stopped dead in the middle of the arena. I thought about dismounting, but didn't. His hooves anchored us squarely to the earth. He closed his eyes. Most horses would panic in that chaos. The crazy energy swirled around us, but I felt safe, peaceful, and loved. It was as if we became one with the earth. He surrendered to nature in complete faith and trust. It was a powerful moment and brought tears to my eyes. About ten minutes later, the storm passed. Frescoe opened his eyes and we resumed our lesson as if nothing had happened. I will never forget that day. Frescoe transformed that potentially threatening environment into a safe place.

How to Be a Safe Place

For a successful reinvention, you must trust yourself and others and create a safe environment in which to thrive.

Here are ten tips to help you be a safe place. These apply to individuals navigating a reinvention, solopreneurs, and to anyone leading through change.

1. Check your own energy. How does it feel to be in your own presence? If you're making yourself nervous, that energy will be transmitted to others. You may be seen as a threat. Relax, take a deep breath, exhale, and give yourself what you need. Give yourself grace and take good care of yourself.

2. Create a routine and schedule to give order and structure to your day/week/month.

3. Clarify expectations, deadlines, and boundaries. Clarity gives confidence.

4. Request and acknowledge input. Listen. Ask questions. Encourage feedback. This ensures that all feel valued and accepted. You may not be able to give them exactly what they need, but just listening allows them to be heard and gives you insight. Be sure to get input from yourself; check in with yourself.

5. To improve competence, provide more training, mentorship, or hire an expert.

6. Show up and be visible. Be present at meetings, be available, and honor your commitments. At times during a reinvention, you will want to hide. Hide outside of your commitments. Schedule "hiding" time.

7. Take a step back and go slower if you feel unclear or overwhelmed.

8. Nurture the culture you desire. For example, to build connectedness and unity, hold team lunches or potlucks, create team-building opportunities, share new learning in lunchtime sessions, or support a nonprofit. If you're leading only yourself, create a culture in which you can thrive.

9. Model the way. Be honest and transparent.

10. Connect to the vision and why that vision is important. Don't let the myriad of details distract you from the larger mission.

In the next chapter, we'll discuss how to take your safe self and lead with impact!

Chapter 4

High-Impact Leadership

Leading through a reinvention requires thought and care. It can be stressful and timelines may be tight. Overwhelm and chaos may run you down. Efficiency is key. After working with hundreds of entrepreneurs and executives, I've observed certain patterns of success. I've also noticed this same pattern while working with horses: the best leaders achieve great results while expending the least amount of energy. I call this the high-impact zone. But how do you find the high-impact zone? To better understand what was going on, I created a simple model.

I found that three primary components drive success: a clear vision, positive fuel source, and appropriate action. Vision is your level of clarity on what you'd like to see happen. Fuel is the energy and mindset you bring to the effort. Appropriate action is required to advance and achieve your goal. Vision, fuel, and action are in constant flux during periods of change and require intentional management. High-impact leadership is leadership that balances all three to operate in the high-impact zone. If one area is missing or deficient, results will be compromised. The following diagram illustrates the high-impact leadership approach. The numbers 1, 2, and 3 indicate what can happen if an area is missing or deficient. Ideally, we want to be working in the middle at X. Where do you see yourself?

High-Impact Leadership

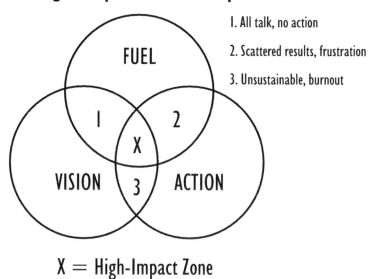

1. All talk, no action

2. Scattered results, frustration

3. Unsustainable, burnout

X = High-Impact Zone

Most leaders are strong in two of the three areas, as noted below.

1—Vision and Fuel: You may be a brilliant visionary able to strategize and build a plan. I've attended many brainstorming, visioning, and strategic planning meetings that left me excited about the future. These meetings can be energizing and serve to unite a team around a common vision. However, the action component is sometimes weak or missing. Creating a vision and strategy without an implementation plan and accountabilities gets you nowhere. You end up in the "all talk, no action" mode. The plan ends up on a shelf or stored in your data files. You get blocked from taking action due to fear, lack of information, lack of prioritization or accountability, or the goal is just too big. Analysis paralysis may set in, and you defer action until a later date. But the later date never comes.

2—Fuel and Action: You may be positive, focused on tasks, and a great action-taker. You get a lot done, and your team loves you. However, you may be so busy tending to daily tasks and crises that the vision or bigger picture of where you're going may be blurry, missing, or not top of mind. Your results are scattered—sometimes successful, sometimes not. This causes frustration.

3—Vision and Action: You may have a strong and clear vision of where you're headed and be taking a lot of action to meet it. However, your fuel source is weak or negative. Leaders begin to burn out from the unyielding pace of the work and constant demands. Staff may leave. Fast-growing organizations and high-pressure environments are especially susceptible to burnout and retention issues. Clear boundaries, delegation, and recharge opportunities must be created for long-term sustainability.

Once you understand where you are, you can make adjustments to get to X. Getting to the high-impact zone is a leadership dance around vision, fuel, and action. Sometimes only a few tweaks are required, other times a full overhaul is necessary. With intention, anyone can reach X.

Using the high-impact leadership approach, several clients achieved top profits, one reorganized a struggling department into an award-winning performer, others gained new market share, another started a new business that was immediately profitable, many secured new senior leadership positions, and two sold their firms. All claimed that they felt more calm and happy than they had in years. Using this approach, I created a thriving business that I love, built the equestrian facility of my dreams (even after the bank rejected part of our construction loan midway through the build), and Lemon Squeezy strolled over a long crinkly tarp like he was walking in his field. The approach works for all goals, personal and professional.

In my sessions with horses, high-impact leadership results in everyone being "in step." The humans' and horse's steps synchronize. This happens automatically as everyone "steps" into a shared vision with trusting energy and walks forward together. The synchronized footfall represents the team's alignment and emerges organically. I only noticed this when observing photos following our sessions. It's pretty remarkable.

Let's take a closer look at the components of the model and discuss how to get to X. Then Lemon Squeezy will show us what it takes to lead through change.

Vision

One of the top keys to success is the ability to see your goal achieved. What's your goal? What do you want? Can you envision it?

During a reinvention, there are many moving parts. It's important to hold both a long-term vision of your goal and a near-term vision for what you want to achieve each day. On some days, you may need to laser in on each moment to stay on track. Focus requires discipline to avoid unnecessary distractions. As I've learned from working with horses, clarity is key. If you're not clear on what you want, you will not get it.

For example, one day I was in a retail shop and the owner and I started chatting. She expressed her struggles with her business and began to share her challenges. I asked her, "What do you want?" She looked stunned. "In what sense?" she asked. I rephrased my question, "How would it look if everything was going well?" I asked for details. She paused and said, "More customers, but I guess I don't know specifically. I hadn't thought about that." I found out that she had been a competitive horse rider years ago. I asked her what would happen if she wasn't clear with a horse on what she wanted. She began to smile. I wished her well and left with my merchandise.

If you can see it, you can make it happen. If you're not clear about what you want, you may get tossed to the ground or swirl around in a sea of confusion. I've been tossed to the ground. It hurts. Here are three ways to develop a vision.

BE INTENTIONAL

One of the best ways to gain clarity and "see" your goal is to practice setting an intention. High-impact leadership requires you to initiate and lead. It is a proactive process. Many of us work in a reactive mode. It can be easier to respond than initiate.

To be more proactive, ask yourself, What is my intention? Consider this question throughout the day and notice what happens. Then expand it out in time: What is my intention for the year? What is my intention for the next three years? Pondering these questions will prompt your brain to search for possibilities. As possibilities arise, notice the ones you're attracted to. Then ask yourself, "What could that look like?"

USE VISUALIZATION

Create a vision board or imagine what you desire. Look at it every day. Viewing a vision board or holding an image in your mind triggers your brain's reticular activating system (RAS). The RAS helps filter and prioritize sensory information and focus on what you want. You'll begin to see opportunities and pursue relationships in alignment with your goals. Animals use the RAS to search out and capture prey. Humans can use the RAS to help "capture" a goal.

Brainstorm with yourself, your leadership team, and/or others you trust. Explore different visions, experiment and discover. Make the brainstorming session light and fun. You don't have to figure it out all at once. Allow a vision to emerge and evolve. Consider the following questions:

a) What's my best work so far?

b) What do I want to continue?

c) What would add more value?

d) What else would my clients love?

e) What could it look like?

f) What would it feel like?

g) What would my clients say once we achieve it?

h) How would it affect my life?

I first used the power of visualization when I was ten years old. I wanted a new bike. My small banana-seat two-wheeler wasn't cutting it anymore, and I knew exactly what I wanted—a shiny blue five-speed with black-and-white trim. It was sitting in the window of my favorite shop, but my family couldn't afford it. That summer, my parents shipped my sister and me off to our grandparents in New York, a fair distance away from the bike. But I was determined to get that bike. I drew a picture of it and hung it over my bed at my grandparents' house. I looked at it constantly and dreamed of speeding down hills with my dog Maggie and my best friend. I didn't know how I'd get that bike, but I knew it was mine. Then my grandfather offered me a job at his drugstore helping to stock shelves and price products. I stocked shelves with glee and carefully penned prices on everything from sunscreen to beach balls. At the end of the summer, I almost had enough money to buy that bike. My parents graciously donated the difference, and I sprinted to the store.

Little did I know then that I would use this same process (with a few more tactical details) throughout my life.

IMAGINE YOUR BEST-CASE SCENARIO

What if you achieved your perfect life? A perfect blend of work and play. Can you consider that possibility? Many cannot. Consider these questions to help open your imagination, tap into your creativity, and see possibilities. Remember, you are only doing this in your mind; there is no risk!

a) What is your best-case scenario? Notice how easy or difficult it is to answer this question. Does your mind keep going back to "I'd like to, but…" or "Oh, but I could never do that"? Those are limiting beliefs, which we'll discuss in the fuel section. For now, remove the perceived limiting factor—money, time, age, whatever—from the picture. Allow yourself to dream without limitations and judgment.

b) What if you said yes to the best-case scenario? Did your heart just skip a beat? Did you suddenly feel nervous? Check in with your heart and gut. Your body is giving you information. How does pondering this question feel? Does it excite you, terrify you, excite and terrify you? That's good. You are waking up to possibilities and considering them as real.

c) What would need to shift if you said yes to the best-case scenario? Here's where your rational mind can jump back in. It can help you begin to outline a plan in your mind.

d) What resources would you need to make the best-case scenario a reality? Yes, most everyone could use a bit more time and money, but here's where you begin drilling down to the details. Look around in your imagination. What specifically do you need—a new website, a new hire, a new building, a new job, subcontractor support, a dog walker, a housecleaner, a coach, investors?

After you've identified what you want, it's time to check your fuel.

Fuel

Fuel is your energy from moment to moment. Your energy consists of your beliefs, thoughts, emotions, and experiences. It influences your perspective, how you feel, your decisions, your actions, and how others feel about you. Your energy is also affected by your physical health. Be sure to nourish yourself well to optimize your fuel.

Your energy is an invisible and silent superpower. It can work for you and against you. Whether you know it or not, you are constantly sharing it with the world. Others judge you by how they feel when they are around you. Think about some people you know. How do you feel in their presence? Do they make you feel happy, neutral, or a bit anxious? Our bodies pick up information when we're in the presence of another or a group. Good leaders pay attention to this energy and alter it to create productive environments.

There are two types of energy that drive behavior: fear and love. Fear includes anxiety and doubt. Love includes confidence and trust. Neutral energy is a form of love energy that I discussed a lot in *Take the Reins! 7 Secrets to Inspired Leadership*. In neutral energy, you are calm, present, and aware without judgment. You just be.

Fear can keep you safe and push you into action. It's is a great short-term motivator. But chronic fear causes stress and reduces your quality of life. Too much fear can block you from achieving your goals and your ability to reach the high-impact zone. Fear may push away what you most desire. Love, confidence, and trust enhance your quality of life and help attract what you most desire.

Over time, chronic fear can drain you and leave you exhausted. Love recharges you. You can think of fear and love as debits and credits from your personal energy bank account. Fear withdraws energy from your account (-); love deposits energy in your account (+). For these reasons, I consider fear negative energy and love positive energy. You need to be sure you have enough positive energy to achieve your goals.

When you are aware of your energy, you can shift it to inspire different thoughts, behaviors, and results for yourself and your team. Once you begin to use your fuel source with intention, you can empower your life. You make better decisions, build deeper connections, take better action, and hone skills in observation, listening, and inquiry. Your life gains more meaning. Any superpower must be handled with great respect. Empower positive fuel and give yourself what you need to keep it flowing. Here's how.

HOW TO EMPOWER POSITIVE FUEL

Strengthen your positive fuel "muscle" as you would any muscle—practice and work it. You can do this without working up a sweat. My favorite activities for empowering positive fuel include a daily practice of gratitude, affirmations, and meditation. I also practice switching negative fear-based thoughts to more productive thoughts.

These activities direct your brain to focus on the positive. When your brain finds something good, it releases dopamine, oxytocin, or serotonin. Neuroscience calls these the "feel-good chemicals" since they help us to feel good. The better you feel, the more positive your fuel. Let's look at each activity.

Gratitude. Developing a daily gratitude practice is simple. Every night before you fall asleep (or in the morning), think about three things that you are grateful for from that day. This makes your brain search the events of the day for something good. Be sure to anchor your gratitude to specifics from that day. Avoid rote recitation. For example, "I am grateful to have met so many inspiring people at today's event," or, "I am so grateful to my knees for feeling strong on today's run." If you're having a rough day, you may want to challenge yourself to find twenty or more things you are grateful for.

Affirmations. To create a powerful affirmation, think about a peak experience. A peak experience is a time when you felt fantastic. It can be work-related or non-work related, but it must be significant to you. For example, perhaps you gave a compelling speech, completed a marathon, traveled alone to another country, secured a fantastic new job, hiked a tall mountain, presented research to a board, or received an award. Think about who you were in that moment and create three affirmations based on that experience. Use present tense. For example, "I am strong. I am committed. I am a great communicator." This is who you are at your best. Try out different statements, use other sentence structures, and feel which ones inspire you. Declare your affirmations each day in front of the mirror. This may sound silly, but it works. For example, one of my peak experiences was galloping over fences with my horse Dixie during a competition. She cleared every jump with ease. As we raced to the finish line, I beamed with pride. She had been a tough horse to train, and I fell off her many times. My affirmations from that experience are "I am trusted. I am free. I can fly." These statements still feel true and bring me great joy.

Meditation. Meditation is a great way to clear your mind. Sit in silence for a few minutes each day. This gives your mind an opportunity to relax and reset. If you are new to meditation, start with short sessions up to five minutes. Don't force anything and don't judge yourself. As thoughts arise, notice the thought and allow it to pass. I like to sit outside near our wetland. Sometimes I don't meditate; I just sit and observe nature.

Walking meditation is another way to clear your mind. Walk slowly, take deliberate steps, and notice your breathing. Allow your breaths to be long and slow.

I do a form of meditation when I first get on a horse. As we walk, I match my breathing to its footfall. I count the horse's steps as I breathe in and out. Depending on the horse, this may be eight counts of in-breath and eight counts of out-breath. This clears my mind and helps us both relax and find a rhythm. Often the horse's steps get longer and slower.

Switch your thoughts. The "Thinking Path" exercise is a process of inquiry to help you intentionally switch from one thought to another. This is very useful for shifting from a negative thought to something more positive. The exercise includes four questions:[5]

1) What am I thinking?

2) How does that make me feel?

3) How does it make me behave or what does it make me do?

4) What is the result of that behavior/action?

If the result of the thought does not feel empowering, ask yourself, "How else can I think about this?" Then go through the process again to find a different result. Do this a few times to find a thought that helps you to move forward.

Now it's time to take action!

Action

To reach the high-impact zone, you must take the right kind of action. Not all action is equal. Many people waste time doing unnecessary tasks, like scrolling through endless emails, constantly checking social media, and attending unproductive meetings. Be aware when you gravitate toward these familiar actions. This is a sign that you might be avoiding the unfamiliar out of fear. It's easy to take action that gets you nowhere. Being "busy" is not necessarily productive.

But sometimes taking any action is better than doing nothing. It may not be high impact, but the action can give you confidence. You don't have to have your fuel all perfect to move forward. You may feel scared, but if you take action, you begin to feel better. That action helps your fuel to shift, and you begin to take better action. Your next action could be a high-impact action. Give yourself grace in this process and do the best you can.

Taking high-impact action requires intention, focus, listening, and clear boundaries. Here's how to do it.

HOW TO TAKE HIGH-IMPACT ACTION

High-impact action is action that achieves results with the least amount of effort. For example, one conversation with the right person at the right time can give you the opportunity of a lifetime. Relationships are key. Your top priorities for action must include creating and deepening relationships, understanding and antic-ipating needs, delivering top-quality service, and being a trusted resource. This is true whether you're a solopreneur or small-business owner, leading a corporate team, or reinventing.

I see three main areas where many of us struggle:

1. Creating offerings before understanding what the target market really wants, needs, and is willing to pay for. We assume we know what they want. We spend time designing programs and offerings, creating beautiful websites and outreach materials, but we haven't talked with one person in our target market.

2. Getting so consumed supporting one client that we do not make time to pipeline new prospects. If that one client pulls out, we're left scrambling.

3. Responding to a prospect or client request before having a full conversation about needs. This can lead to a massive missed opportunity or much time wasted redoing work.

I have personal experience in all three of those areas. The school of hard knocks is expensive. But I've also learned a few things.

For example, years ago I received a call for potential leadership coaching. The prospect had received two quotes from other coaches and wanted a third bid. We talked in-depth, and after a few minutes, it became obvious that she was dealing with a complex issue that might require more than leadership coaching. I asked if she would be willing to meet in person. She said yes and mentioned that none of the other coaches had requested more detail or a meeting. I ended up supporting her and her organization for several years. She received the full support needed to move forward.

Here are a few guiding questions to help you focus your action. Check in with your vision first. Then go take action.

1. What are the three most important things that must be done today to advance the vision?

2. Is this the best use of my time or could someone else do this faster/better?

3. What relationship(s) must be nurtured? (team member, strategic partner, vendor, client, prospect, board member, etc.)

4. What am I setting up for the future? (For example, speaking events, new programs/offerings, a plan to bid on a contract, stronger prospect pipeline.) What needs to be done to prepare?

5. Who needs to know about me/my work? Set up meetings with key players inside and outside of your firm to raise awareness. Build credibility by writing articles, blog posts, and giving talks.

6. What baby step can I take right now to advance the vision? Completing baby steps builds confidence and momentum.

7. What energy drains must be eliminated? Energy drains are anything that drains your energy. This may include open decisions, outstanding invoices, underperforming programs or departments, overdue healthcare appointments, or anything that is waiting for a response from you. This can include ridding yourself of toxic people.

8. Who else can help? No top performer works alone. Reach out to your team and find trusted experts to support your goal. If you work by yourself, join a mastermind, form referral partnerships, get a coach, hire experts, or invest in a program to help you move forward.

Note: Sometimes the best action is to take no action. Take a break. Rest is critical to advance. Refuel.

Now let's see what high-impact leadership looks like with Lemon Squeezy.

High-Impact Leadership with Lemon Squeezy

In session two of Reinvention in the Round, we simulated a scenario in which Lemon Squeezy and I would review requirements for a $10 million request for proposal (RFP). The goal was to decide if he would lead the proposal development. We called this the "tarp proposal," which was represented by a 16-foot-long gray tarp. Lemon Squeezy was loose in the arena, now an imaginary conference room. To review the RFP requirements,

I unrolled the tarp. The crinkly fabric's loud sounds and shifting shape scared Lemon Squeezy. He took off cantering around the ring, his eyes wide, his veins bulging. He raced around for a few minutes. I continued to review the requirements myself. But by the end of session two, he and I stood shoulder to shoulder and stared down at the edge of the tarp. The audience and I agreed that this meant he would think about leading it.

The next month during session three of Reinvention in the Round, we simulated a meeting to follow up with Lemon Squeezy. I wanted to know if we were moving forward with him as the proposal lead. We entered the "conference room." He was free to go wherever he chose. He walked by my side as we weaved in and out around two red exercise balls, blue barrels, and orange cones. It was as if we were brainstorming strategies. Then I walked to the corner and pulled out the tarp proposal. I dragged it behind me and he followed closely. As I unrolled the proposal, he stood quietly by my side. I walked down the middle of the long tarp and he followed without hesitation. His hooves smacked against the vinyl in rhythm with my feet. The audience was awestruck. We agreed that Lemon Squeezy was comfortable with the RFP requirements and had said yes to leading the proposal.

What changed from session two to session three? I did not train him on the tarp between sessions.

Here's what happened: we were in the high-impact zone. We had a good blend of a clear vision, positive fuel, and appropriate action. By empowering Lemon Squeezy to decide for himself if he was comfortable with the RFP requirements, he did not feel pressured. He trusted me to trust him. I was clear on what would be expected—a walk across the tarp—but never once did I force him to do that. He did it on his own. Lemon Squeezy felt safe, explored options, took risks, and grew into this leadership role in a very short time. The photos from this session showed that our footfall was synchronized as we walked together over the tarp. It's amazing what can happen in the high-impact zone.

Summary Tips to Lead Yourself and Others Through Change

1. Be clear on the destination, the vision of your goal achieved.

2. Check your fuel source, your energy. Are you leading from a place of confidence and trust or fear? Fear drives others away and incites stress and volatility. Calm confidence generates trust and openness. Shift your energy as needed.

3. Address uncertainties. Be honest with yourself and your team. Identify potential risks. Listen to their fears. Address your own fears. Take a step back if needed.

4. Clarify roles and responsibilities. During change, roles and responsibilities may shift. This may result in promotions, lateral moves, and natural attrition. Be clear on expectations and new procedures.

5. Allow your team members to choose to step forward into the new. Not everyone will embrace change, and some may choose to leave the organization. Communicate regularly. Stay close to your team and encourage them to do the same with their managers and staff. Share updates and timelines, and celebrate small wins. This builds trust and engagement and assures the team that progress is underway.

Chapter 5

How to Make Great Decisions

We have all been taught how to weigh pros and cons when making a decision. If the pros outweigh the cons, you can move forward with some certainty that the decision is a good one. It's a rational and proven approach and one I've used many times. But in pursuit of my passion and purpose, I've thrown those cons right out the window many times. I was determined to let nothing hold me back. That was not a good idea. It took me seven years to recover from a couple of risky decisions that left me financially, physically, and emotionally broken (we'll talk about that in the resilience chapter). Now I'm a bit more savvy.

Now I use a different approach. I tap into my entire "being" to make a decision. My entire being includes my core values, love, and body wisdom. As a final check, I challenge my thoughts. This gives me a much higher degree of confidence that my decision is the right one. You can use this approach to supplement weighing pros and cons. Here's how it works.

Identify Your Core Values

Your core values are your guiding principles. They are unique to you and shape your perspective and behavior. When used with intention, they are a powerful aid in decision-making.

Here's a short list of some common values.

Example Common Values	
• Health	• Creativity
• Fairness	• Tolerance
• Flexibility	• Joy
• Honesty	• Stability
• Integrity	• Gratitude
• Freedom	• Accuracy
• Balance	• Courage
• Learning	• Connection
• Achievement	• Innovation
• Growth	• Independence

Take a moment to brainstorm and list your values. Why are they important to you? How do they feel in your body? When I consider values, I may feel a quiet certainty, or my heart gives a resounding "yes." If there is no resonance in my body, the value is not a top value.

Review your list and identify your top five. Be selective and only choose five. Write them down. These are your core values.

Check every decision against these values. For example, let's say you are considering a career move and your core values are "independence, innovation, creativity, growth, and achievement." You are grappling between two choices: (1) running a start-up firm or (2) running a department at a large established organization with a lot of bureaucracy. At first glance, number one may be a better fit for your core values. Knowing your core values gives you insight to ask more questions about number two. This helps you make a better informed decision.

Knowing your core values can also help in building a business. If stability, fairness, and tolerance are some of your core values, be sure you create a culture that honors those same values. Consider what "stability" would look like in that company and design accordingly. For example, perhaps position yourself to serve as a subcontractor on long-term projects while you build your prospect pipeline. Develop standard operating procedures and ensure adherence.

Be sure to check in with your core values periodically, since they may change. What you held dear ten years ago may not be as significant now.

For example, one client owned a popular martial arts studio for many years. He loved his work, but business growth pressures were intensifying and he struggled between making more investments and spending more time on his other passion, his art. After much contemplation, he realized that he valued stability and freedom. He wanted to be able to give more time to painting. He closed his business and was hired by a resort. The resort made him its artist-in-residence. His work is now featured all over the world.

My core values now include "freedom, authenticity, connection, service, and kindness," but years ago "achiever" was one of my core values. Achiever drove me to make decisions that would support getting ahead in my career and passions. I held multiple jobs simultaneously to increase my income and attended graduate school while working full-time. At 25, I bought a townhouse as an investment. I took riding lessons from top professionals, and researched and purchased the best-crafted equipment I could to support my passion. I wanted to be a high-level competitor.

Someone recently asked me my goals for Lemon Squeezy. I pondered for a moment. Now my goals are a peaceful happy partnership where we can go on relaxing trail rides and play with dressage and jumping. We may compete, we may not. I really don't care. I just like him and enjoy spending time learning together. My "connection and freedom" core values drive many of my decisions. I am also still committed to being the best horseman I can be and study all the time to hone those skills and raise my riding ability. Achiever is still a value, but it's not a core value.

Follow the Love

I developed the "follow the love" triangle approach to help clients figure out how to best spend their time and energy. It's great for identifying your primary area of service, target market, ideal clients, and where to provide pro bono support. It can also be used for anything in life. It has three sides:

1. Do what you love,

2. For those who you love to serve/work with/be around,

3. Who greatly appreciate you.

Follow the LOVE!

Who Greatly Appreciate You

Of course, this requires that you spend some time pondering what you love and who you love to serve. When I am invited to engage on projects, I ask myself, "Do I love this? Do I 'love' these people? Would they care that I'm spending time doing this?" If the answers are anything but yes, I need to take a hard look at why I'm spending time on it. Your time and energy are your most valuable resources. Be picky!

Love and gratitude fuel your soul and are powerful motivators in business. Using the "follow the love" approach ensures that you are engaging in activities that propel you forward and sustain you for the long term.

This approach is especially useful for making decisions on how to spend discretionary time. Leaders always get requests to join nonprofits, serve on boards, give talks, be part of industry groups, and donate time. Be sure that you spend this time supporting something you believe in and that the organization appreciates your efforts. I've been part of a few organizations that barely acknowledge the efforts of volunteers. That does not fuel your soul. I've also made lifelong friendships from pro bono work, and some of it has helped my business gain visibility and new clients.

Body Wisdom

Another way to help make great decisions is to ask your head, heart, and gut for input. Each is a major nerve center. You know how sometimes you have a gut feeling or a gut instinct? That is gut intelligence. Be sure to listen. I talked about head, heart, gut decision-making a bit in my previous book. Since then, new research has been conducted that shows the connections between these centers. Here's a brief summary.

The brain in your head is your rational center and contains 100 billion neurons. Your heart is your feeling center and contains 40,000 neurons. Your gut, also known as your enteric nervous system, is your intuition and contains 100 million neurons. Research shows that all are connected by the vagus nerve, which sends information throughout these three areas to help regulate activities such as breathing and heart rate, blood pressure, digestion, and how we feel emotionally and physically.

The HeartMath Institute (HMI) found that the heart emits the largest electromagnetic field of any of the body's organs and can be sensed several feet away from the physical body. This field carries information which can influence communication. Anyone who has felt love knows the intense power of the heart. Research conducted by Dr. Rollin McCraty, HMI's Director of Research, shows that when we are emotionally upset, we tend to make poor decisions; but when the heart is calm, we make better decisions.[6] Research is ongoing.[7]

Research has also shown that the gut "talks" to the brain and can influence how we feel. Studies show that the head-gut neural pathway is linked to both anxiety and digestion issues. Some gastroenterologists have prescribed antidepressants for patients with irritable bowel syndrome (IBS) to help calm IBS symptoms. According to Dr. Jay Pasricha, Director of the Johns Hopkins Center for Neurogastroenterology, research is being conducted on the potential power of cognitive behavioral therapy to help heal gastric disorders.[8]

A 2018 study conducted by Dr. Wenfei Han, Assistant Professor of Neuroscience at the Icahn School of Medicine at Mount Sinai, showed that the vagus nerve sends information from the gut to the reward center in the brain in our head which releases dopamine, a neurotransmitter that makes us feel good. More research is being conducted to further understand these important communication pathways.[9]

Bringing your awareness to sensations in your head, heart, and gut can give you powerful insights.

To make a decision using head, heart, and gut, think of a question that can be answered yes or no. Take a deep breath and slowly exhale. Settle yourself. Then, one at a time, ask each nerve center for a response.

Wait patiently. This can take practice. Some people are able to feel their heart but not their gut; others feel their gut but not their heart. The head response is usually loud since it gets a lot of practice.

Ideally, you want agreement between all three nerve centers. If you reach agreement, you can be pretty certain that you have a solid decision, a "yes" or "no." Sometimes you get a "maybe." You may also get a "not yet." If you get a "maybe" or "not yet," ask that nerve center what else would be needed to make a decision. Perhaps more information or more time would be helpful.

Listen carefully. Your heart knows what it wants, and so does your gut. If you can't hear or feel a response, practice with easier decisions, ones that you already know in your head. Allow yourself to feel the response in the heart and gut. Do this regularly and you will begin to feel these areas more easily.

Challenge Your Thinking: Why Not BOTH?

As a final check, I challenge my thinking. Decisions are influenced by what you assume and believe to be possible. Many of us assume that to have one thing means we have to give up or sacrifice another. This is "either/or" thinking and can close down the options you see. Instead, consider if having/doing both could be possible. This is "both/and" thinking. It expands your perspective and opens more options and insights. It may not be possible to have or do both fully, but perhaps you can have a little of each.

For example, maybe you'd like to quit your day job to start the business you've always desired, but the fear of sacrificing income and benefits stops you from taking action. That's a valid fear. Start-ups can take time to generate income. But this is either/or thinking. Instead, think about how you may be able to do both. How can you begin to get set up for a future venture while at your existing job? What do you need? Who do you need to meet? What credibility do you need to build? Start writing a business plan. Make appointments outside of work time to meet people. Attend conferences and networking events in that industry or on that topic. If you are an expert in this area already, write articles or blogs to share your expertise and be seen. Create a business card and draft a website. You can do all of this while working your day job. This is both/and thinking. It's a compromise strategy that advances your goals while mitigating risk. Eventually you may feel ready to launch your new business full-time.

You can also use this approach for personal goals. For example, let's say you want to run a marathon but you've been a couch potato for ten years, you work full-time, and you have small children. Just the thought of running 26.2 miles is exhausting, so you put off training and do nothing. The thinking is: *I can either be a full-time working mother or I can be an athlete and run a marathon.* Instead, perhaps consider what it would take to prepare for a one-mile race. You know you can do a one-mile race. You can probably walk it right now. Perhaps you can train with your kids. Perhaps it could be fun? Considering this possibility expands your thinking, opens new options, and gives you an opportunity to make a decision to move forward.

There is an extensive body of work on both/and thinking called polarity thinking. It is beyond the scope of this book, but I encourage anyone with an interest to check out the work of Dr. Barry Johnson and Cliff Kayser at Polarity Partnerships to dive deeper.[10]

Putting It into Practice with Lemon Squeezy

When I thought about buying Lemon Squeezy, my heart was screaming "YES," my gut said a more quiet "yes," and my head said, "Are you crazy?"

My head also shared a lot of other thoughts, like "You're not good enough to have a young green horse like that," "You don't have time for a project like that," "You'll get hurt with a horse like that." Some of those thoughts had merit. I did have to up my skills and I did have to and still have to carve out the time. Working around horses, even quiet horses, can be dangerous. I accept that risk. On the positive side, creating a business program around his reinvention would help other professionals facing similar changes. That opportunity served well beyond my riding needs and met my core values. The potential rewards outweighed the risks.

When I decided to leave my last corporate job, I also used these decision-making approaches. My head struggled with the practicalities of resigning from a well-paying job with lots of autonomy and a great team. It told me I was jumping off a cliff to a certain demise. The fear was enormous. My heart and gut yelled "YES!" The opportunity aligned with my core values and strengths, but I waited for a year before leaving my corporate job to do more research and give my head time to feel better. My head still panicked when I cut the tie, but it recovered.

Here are a few questions to consider when making decisions:

1. How important is this? Why is it important? Why else? Keep asking this question until you feel some strong emotions. That's the truth.

2. What are the risks of pursuing it?

3. What if I didn't do it?

4. What if I fail? Of course we know there is no such thing as failure, just "opportunities for growth." But get real here; sometimes things don't work out. You need to address this possibility. I tend to forget to ask myself this question, but it's critical for a full assessment.

5. What do I need to do to minimize risk and be safe?

6. Does a yes align with my core values?

7. Will I love doing this?

8. Will it help those who I best serve/care about?

9. Will they appreciate it?

10. How does this feel in my head, heart, gut?

11. What am I assuming about this?

12. Is this an either/or decision or is some sort of "both" possible?

Making a decision will give you great relief. But after you make a decision, you may face some new unexpected challenges or "opportunities for growth." You may confront an identity crisis. We'll address this in the next chapter.

Chapter 6

The Identity Crisis

We use labels to characterize and make sense of the world. Labels identify you and others; for example, "I'm a lawyer," "He's an accountant," "My sister is an artist," or, "She owns a software company." When we hear these labels, we make assumptions about education, lifestyle, and even status and wealth. This is a dangerous game, since much of the time assumptions are inaccurate at best. But we do it anyway. Labels box the various aspects of life into tidy little packages and give us a sense of comfort and understanding.

One of the biggest challenges of reinvention is dealing with identity uncertainty. When you're reinventing, your identity is evolving. Answering "What do you do?" may be a struggle. Contemplating "Who am I?" is even worse.

During a reinvention, who you are right now may not be who you want to be or how you see yourself. Who you were in the past may seem irrelevant to who you want to be. You may not fit in any box. This can be confusing and frustrating. It can also be quite liberating. Who are you without all the labels? It took me several attempts to sort this out for my own reinventions.

A few of my clients have assumed leadership positions following the retirement of a long-time leader. This can be especially challenging. You must measure up. Your style may be radically different from the previous leader. It can take time to find your groove and be accepted, respected, and trusted. It may also take your new team time to adjust to you. This can shake your confidence and make you question your identity. Who are you in this new space? It's also an opportunity to be better than you ever were before.

In this chapter, I'll share a couple of my own identity challenges, and Lemon Squeezy will share his view. Then we'll look at some ways to make peace with your evolving identity.

My First Identity Crisis

I was an environmental scientist for 20 years and strongly identified with that role. To me, it meant I was analytical, cared about nature, enjoyed the outdoors, and was committed to a cause bigger than myself. In most circles, I was respected for my profession. I was also an emerging entrepreneur with a need to explore and create. I was drawn to the excitement of starting something new.

When the information technology (IT) industry blossomed in our area, I jumped at an opportunity to join the frenzy. I resigned from my career to start an IT staffing firm, a new division of my family's small business in California.

I launched into the work with great enthusiasm, but I struggled with my new identity and the business development approach used by most in that industry, the cold call. Back then, success was a numbers game—the more calls you made, the more likely it was to close a deal. I carefully crafted my script and began dialing. The calls did not go well. My friendly opening greeting was met with curt responses, some disrespectful. A few people hung up on me. The "salesperson" label came with a lot of negative associations. This was so disorienting, since I was still the same person with the same commitment to excellence, service, and quality as I had been as an environmental scientist. The only thing that had changed was the role. Or was that all?

In fact, my perception of myself had shifted. I had doubts about whether this new role was a good fit and I struggled with the calls. With each rejection, I began to lose confidence. The sales concept of "every no is one step closer to a yes" felt foreign and insincere.

I had to make some shifts or get a new job. To succeed, I had to figure out how to be in this new space. Who was I? I wasn't sure.

After some deep soul searching, I found that I was trying to conform to an approach that didn't work for me, although others used cold calling with great success. I had never used a script for anything in my life, and I tend to do things my own way. Not being "good" in this role was torture. I was used to being successful. One of my best strengths was connecting with others. But I wasn't connecting. In fact, others were hanging up on me, a literal and metaphorical disconnect. The irony was humbling.

I realized that my insecurities were driving my cold calls and driving away business. Fear-based energy consumed me, yet I was using it to try to grow this business—of course I was failing. I took a deep breath, threw out my script, and began to focus solely on what could best help a prospect.

I looked back over what had worked for me in the past. I had led teams and directed projects and even overseen a few software development efforts. Years before, I had taken a class in the lifecycle management process of software development. I knew the extreme pressures of getting a software release out on time, hopefully bug-free. Mostly I went deep. I learned as much as I could about a few firms and joined an industry association. I became a member of the board and developed relationships. Instead of making many calls, I made calls to a few firms and secured meetings with decision-makers. As I gained confidence, I had heartfelt honest conversations with prospects about their needs. I developed trust. People said, "You don't sound like a salesperson." Good, I wasn't. I finally began to reclaim my true identity.

I also focused my niche. At first, I was trying to serve all parts of the IT industry, a classic case of "fear of missing out." I realized that my fear of missing out was causing me to miss out on everything. So, I determined which part of the industry I most enjoyed and focused on that. I enjoyed helping businesses conduct online transactions, or e-portal development, as it was known back then. Within six months, we were locally known as the firm to see for staffing support in that niche. We generated $2.1 million in sales in six months mostly by referral, not cold calls.

My identity crisis took some time to sort out. During a reinvention, it can be difficult to let go of an old identity and open to the new. Sometimes you forget your strengths, transferable experience, and what works best for you.

Another Identity Crisis

You may have more than one identity crisis. I had another when I shifted careers from being a director at an environmental engineering firm to my current role.

Before I opened my practice, I worked privately with a business coach. I also received coaching in a group. I thought I was ready. I had the expertise and background, but my identity crisis almost sank me again.

When I opened my new practice, I introduced myself as a management consultant, a vague term that means nothing to the general public, but sounded cool. In that same introduction, I also talked about how I had been an environmental scientist for twenty years and now focus on business strategy. What? Why would one buy business strategy from an environmental scientist? How confusing for the other party. Most people would nod politely and begin to drift across the room before I remembered to share about my strong business background. I would kick myself all the way home.

Other times I called myself a coach and gave a spiel about optimizing performance. That's true, but quite bland. Although I am a coach, I do many other things; coaching is one method I use in my work. So is "coach" an identity or one of many tools? My value proposition needed work.

To further complicate my identity, sometimes I would introduce myself by saying that I partnered with horses for business transformation. That's true and a differentiator, but it focuses on the modality of the work, not on the issues that I help to address or the outcomes we achieve. But it did get their attention. I did that a few too many times and became known as the "horse lady" in some circles. I think some people even thought I was a horse trainer. Who the heck was I? And why was I hanging on to all those labels? I had a lot to sort out.

The truth is that I am all those things. We are all complex beings composed of our past experiences, passions, hopes, and desires. We don't fit in tidy little boxes. That's okay. The simple fix is to shed what is no longer needed, bring forward what best serves the new, and focus on providing valuable service to others. During this process, you learn new ways of serving others while you enjoy life. Once you begin to focus on how you can best serve others, everything becomes more clear.

The fix: I focused on service and not on myself. I let go of my ego. I wrote pro bono articles for the local paper on personal branding, interviewing, and tips for business success. I volunteered as part of a business assistance team. I developed relationships and trust. I began offering free seminars on business topics to help small businesses grow. People showed up. The rest is history.

Footnote to my story: In January 2019, I finally recycled my old graduate school science texts from 1995. A little part of me had been hanging on to that identity for a really long time. Those books served as "proof" of my value and evidence of my hard work. But their time was up. I took a photo of the shelf, then sent the books to the recycling center.

Lemon Squeezy's Identity Crisis

Lemon Squeezy also experienced an identity crisis. His new career as my riding horse was imposed upon him, kind of like a job transfer or company restructuring. He didn't choose it, although my spiritually-minded friends say he did.

He had been a winning racehorse and knew that job well. His race videos are impressive. A fierce local competitor, he could win from behind or lead all the way. In one race, he was many lengths ahead of the field. He looked proud of his work and held his head high after races.

Lemon Squeezy trained on a track with other horses and lived a very structured life. However, the training he received in that career was the opposite of what I needed for my own safe riding horse. For example, racehorses are trained to pick up speed when you take a hold on the reins. When you pull back, they go faster. Those cues had to be completely retrained.

Racehorses normally train with other horses around. I ride alone most of the time. This can be terrifying for a herd animal used to being ridden with his horse buddies. Racehorses might be allowed to move around while the jockey is tossed on. I like a horse to stand still while I mount. Racehorses are not usually brushed, since their coats are maintained short or clipped to quickly expel heat. They are hosed off after workouts and races. I like to brush and groom. Grooming can be a bonding time.

When I first brought him home, Lemon Squeezy didn't see the value of any of my needs. He made nasty faces, pinned his ears back, and tried to bite me while I brushed. He danced around the mounting block and didn't have a clue when I pulled the reins to try to stop.

None of the training I introduced made any sense to him. I could almost feel him saying, "This is not how we do it. You're wasting so much time!" It reminded me of some experts who get reassigned after a merger or acquisition. They have to adapt to a new way of doing things. In the new environment, tasks may feel awkward and cause resentment. One may lose confidence.

Luckily, Lemon Squeezy is smart, sweet (most of the time), and has a great work ethic. I worked to build his trust out of the saddle and focus on his strengths while teaching him some new approaches. This included a lot of work with a halter and lead rope and also with him free in the arena. After several months working together, the riding was coming together. We could stand at the mounting block, stop, turn, and maintain a steady trot even when I took up the reins. He was reinventing. A new relationship and identity were emerging.

How to Make Peace with an Identity Crisis

It takes time to make peace with an identity crisis. There is no quick fix. Go back to basics and get to know yourself again. Give yourself time to find the rhythm of the new. Here are a few suggestions.

1. Review your strengths and be sure to do something each day that uses them. CliftonStrengths is one tool to assess your top five strengths.[11]

2. How have you been successful in the past? What approaches did you use? Create your own way of doing things. You don't have to do things the way others do. Be yourself. Do "you."

3. Let go of ego and focus on service to others. Build relationships and trust. What are their needs?

4. Review your values and why they are important to you. Be sure your job honors your values.

5. Release labels from your past that do not pertain to the new. Edit them out of your speech. Be present in the now.

6. Give yourself permission to be okay with uncertainty. Release the need to prove anything and allow yourself to learn in this new space. Surrender and accept the current situation. You don't have to figure it out.

7. Practice self-acceptance. I am a big fan of self-help author and publishing giant Louise Hay.[12] She suggested using affirmations to empower healing and self-love. One of my favorites is "I love and accept myself." This is an unconditional statement—your self-acceptance is not conditional. You love and accept yourself right now exactly as you are. Recite this affirmation. How does it feel? Does it feel true? If not, release self-judgment.

8. Reconnect with your "why." Why did you make this change? Why is that important? Remind yourself of your goal, and all of your gifts that you bring to the new.

9. Ask for help—many of us do better with support during a transition. Consider who may be able to help, including friends, family, pastor, counselor, coach, and other experts.

10. Spend time with who and what you love most. This fuels your soul and nourishes you for the long term.

Now let's step forward into the new!

Chapter 7

Smoothing a Bumpy Transition

One of the most exciting times during a reinvention is the day you launch into the new. This is the day you make the "change," the third step in the reinvention process. This is a physical transition step; for example, the day you open your new business, your first day at a new job, the beginning of a new project or contract, or the day you acquire a firm or sell your company. For Lemon Squeezy, it was the day I brought him home.

Some transitions go smoothly. One of my clients sold her firm to someone she'd known for years. Her firm's capabilities and culture aligned well with the mission and vision of the buyer. The deal was fast, clean, and everyone benefited. Another client was hired as CEO of a large organization. It was a great fit.

In contrast, early on in my career I worked for a small company that was acquired by a global engineering firm. The leaders in charge promised that nothing would change except the name of the company. I believed that promise. But within six months, everything at that firm changed—the leadership, the health benefits, the 401(k) plan, and the culture. Stress dominated the mood. Many people left, including me. I was hired by the firm's top competitor.

At another point in my career, I worked for a large organization that acquired a small business to deepen a technical niche. At first everyone was excited about this new company, as it added unique and much desired capabilities to the firm. But within three years, the new business area was defunct—a victim of a lack of infrastructure, onboarding, and integration to support it for the long term.

Even with the best planning and onboarding, a transition can be bumpy. After a couple of weeks of intense planning for Lemon Squeezy's arrival, I thought we were prepared. I was wrong. In this chapter, we'll look at considerations to prepare for a transition, Lemon Squeezy's homecoming adventure, and tips for smoothing the path.

Preparing for the Change

Preparing for a transition involves both physical and emotional considerations. Physical considerations include the physical structures and infrastructure that house your new endeavor. At a minimum, these include office space and equipment, contracts, and standard operating procedures. Emotional considerations include relationships and culture; that is, how you and others feel.

Preparing for the physical is straightforward. Here are a few guiding questions:

1. Where will I do my work?

2. What do I need to do my work? (e.g., computer, desk, chair, phone, wireless, etc.)

3. Who do I need to support me? (e.g., banker, attorney, accountant, marketing person, staff, subcontractors, spouse, etc.)

4. What agreements must be in place? (e.g., salary, contracts)

5. How do I do my work? (e.g., business plan, standard operating procedures, hours of operation, telecommute, on location)

6. What will I produce/offer?

7. Who are my clients?

8. What is my contingency plan?

Preparing for the emotional is less straightforward. Predicting human behavior is tricky. We rarely get it right. Here are a few guiding questions to address the emotional considerations.

1. What are my intentions?

2. What type of culture is in place? Or, what type of culture am I creating?

3. Who needs to know my intent and plan?

4. Who will be affected by my plan?

5. Who do I need buy-in from?

6. How does it look from their perspective? How else? How else? Keep asking yourself this until you run out of ideas.

7. Who may be threatened? Why?

8. How can I make everyone feel safe? (be sure to include yourself)

9. Who will help me during the transition?

Prior to Lemon Squeezy's arrival, we planned for his physical requirements. My husband and I have owned horses for over 25 years and used to run a boarding facility. I also acclimated new horses at other boarding facilities. We felt knowledgeable about how best to make this transition. Our plan was to start him in private turnout to adjust to the new environment and later turn him out with the two other male horses, Frescoe and Noble. Horses are herd animals and seek safety in numbers. Lemon Squeezy had lived in fields with other horses. We were told that he was low on the dominance scale and was not a challenging type. We identified the perfect pasture adjacent to Frescoe and Noble. The horses could touch over the fence and would be able to get to know each other from the safety of their own fields without getting chased.

We also had a contingency plan. We set up another field in case the first field didn't work. We replaced old fence boards, cleared fencelines, and bought a new insulated water trough. We felt prepared and excited to bring Lemon Squeezy home.

But we could not control the weather. It was December. A bitter cold front gusted 40 mph winds the day we picked him up. Horses, frigid cold, and big wind are not a peaceful combination. I was worried.

We had also not planned for something else—a violent, uncharacteristic dominance play that shook me to the core. I had seriously underestimated the emotional considerations.

Lemon Squeezy's First Day

Once you make the change, you must be ready to pivot fast if things don't go as expected. Here's what happened.

We trailered Lemon Squeezy late in the afternoon and arrived home just before dark. I led him to his new stall. He sniffed the sawdust, laid down and rolled, then stood up and began munching hay. Frescoe watched him from the neighboring stall. He is one of our older horses. He is a wise and benevolent leader and would be a good mentor for Lemon Squeezy. Lemon Squeezy seemed quiet and comfortable. Frescoe seemed to accept his new barn mate. I was thrilled. Our "onboarding plan" was working so far.

The next morning, it was about five degrees. I blanketed the horses, tossed hay out in the fields, and turned Lemon Squeezy out in the paddock next to Frescoe and Noble. They touched noses over the fence, squealed, and ran around a bit. This is normal, and after a few minutes they settled down and ate their hay piles. The new arrangement seemed to be working. In fact, each time Frescoe and Noble walked off to hay piles farther away, Lemon Squeezy paced the fenceline to try to be near the other horses. He seemed nervous not being next to them. He paced and paced as we watched. The other horses continued to eat their hay, unbothered by Lemon Squeezy's pacing. Each time Frescoe and Noble came closer to Lemon Squeezy, he relaxed and ate his hay. He wanted to be in the field with the others.

I watched this behavior for a few hours. Lemon Squeezy started trotting up and down the fenceline. He was beginning to work up a sweat under his blanket. When the other horses walked closer, he was calm. Sweating in single-digit temperatures is a dangerous health risk. I wondered if Frescoe and Noble could accept Lemon Squeezy in their field. They seemed very calm, and Frescoe had lived in fields with different horses without incident.

After observing a little longer, my husband and I agreed that it should be fine to put Lemon Squeezy in with Frescoe and Noble. We scattered more big hay piles all over the field to give them plenty of food and avoid competition. In winter, grass is limited; the fields were bare. I opened the gate and let Lemon Squeezy into the field.

The three horses touched noses. White puffs of breath rose from their nostrils. For a moment, there was silence. Then Lemon Squeezy squealed and galloped off. Frescoe chased him with Noble in tow. But Frescoe was no match for the ex-racehorse. Hooves thundered on the frozen ground. The horses bucked, spun, and kicked at each other. They skidded and slipped on icy patches. Lemon Squeezy raced on. Then Frescoe tripped and fell to his knees. I watched in horror. He got up slowly and limped across the field. I ran to the barn to get a halter and remove Lemon Squeezy. We had made a terrible mistake.

I caught Lemon Squeezy, put him back in the adjacent field, and ran to tend to Frescoe. Lemon Squeezy galloped around the field in a panic. Sweat streamed down his sides, his blanket was soaked. I thought he was going to crash through the fence. I scurried about and brought all three horses one by one into the barn to settle down and assess the damage. The two mares looked on from their field, unfazed by the dramatic territorial display of testosterone.

I was furious with myself. We've had horses for 19 years on this property and have never had an issue introducing a new horse. We're experienced; we should have read the situation better. But we didn't. We made one mistake; we misjudged. And my sweet Frescoe, who has been with me since his birth, suffered. Of course, it could have gone another way. They could have squealed and settled down to eat hay like they were doing earlier. I felt tremendous guilt. My onboarding plan was a disaster. The situation needed a fix now.

I took a few breaths and reminded myself of who was in charge. The high emotions from the horses had tossed me in a tailspin. I was in charge. I could figure this out. I pondered a solution. We needed to keep the horses separate, but also needed to create a smaller paddock for Lemon Squeezy. This would slow him down a bit and prevent him tearing across the field at a dead run. But you can't build a new fence in frozen ground; the posts can't penetrate. I looked around and spotted some extra metal fencing panels that we use to create a round pen for training horses. Perfect.

My husband and I pulled out the panels and began to create a cross-fence to divide up the paddock. The freezing wind brought the temperature below zero, but we pressed on, determined to fix the situation. It worked. The smaller field reduced the running, and peace prevailed.

Lemon Squeezy still paced the fenceline, but that was a small price to pay for physical safety. Luckily Frescoe was fine after a few days.

None of us could have predicted the territorial challenge Lemon Squeezy presented to Frescoe, or Frescoe's response. Lemon Squeezy is a vibrant athletic young horse who loves to run. Maybe he was just happy to run free and meant no harm. As the herd leader, Frescoe felt compelled to protect Noble and his territory, and to teach Lemon Squeezy the rules, like preserving a work culture. The ground and weather conditions made this a challenge. In the horse world, that's really all that happened. It's normal, and horses usually work it out. If the weather conditions were milder, perhaps all would have been quiet after a few minutes of running.

But I am the ultimate leader. I make decisions for the well-being of the entire herd. If I don't think things are being handled appropriately, I must step in. Frescoe needed support. Even hurting, Frescoe would have continued to impose the rules to be sure Noble was safe. He's also an older horse with physical issues. I couldn't take the chance that he would get seriously injured. So we made some fast changes. Things had not gone as planned, but we recovered.

Remember, you are in control, no matter your position. Plan the transition, make the change, do your best, and be ready to pivot if the situation begins to deteriorate. Keep yourself and your people safe.

The two acquisition stories I mentioned earlier did not trigger effective remedial action on the part of the leadership. They did nothing. Morale suffered. Emotional suffering can be worse than physical suffering. Productivity dropped and potential profits were compromised. Pay attention to your own needs and the needs of your people. Make adjustments and be sure that your solution is working. The worst thing to do is to assume that it will work itself out. Sometimes it will. But at what cost?

If you're jumping off the corporate track to start your own business, congratulations! Know that there may be long days of silence and solitude as you sort out where you need to be and how you work best in the new space. Fill your days with relationship-building opportunities. Stay engaged to stave off the isolation. Be flexible and open to new opportunities.

Here are a few tips to smooth the path.

Tips to Smooth the Path

You are responsible for your own experience. Do not let others steal your power or dictate your path. Give yourself what you need and be aware of the needs of others. Here are ten tips.

1. Learn before you leap—review physical and emotional considerations.

2. Prepare and control what you can, release what you cannot.

3. Take action and do your best.

4. Remember to breathe.

5. Assume nothing and watch carefully.

6. Be ready to pivot.

7. Forgive yourself and others—give yourself grace in the space.

8. Get help.

9. Regroup.

10. Continue to move forward.

If at some point you feel like you're beginning to hit a wall, buckle your seat belt and read on.

Chapter 8

I Can't Do This! Break Down to Break Through

"Don't give up on me!" a little voice yelled in my head as the bay horse raced around the arena bucking and pulling on the rope. What the heck? Where did that voice come from? Was it mine? Was it his? I didn't know. I did know that what was happening was far from the peaceful and fun partnership I had envisioned. This behavior had been going on for weeks. I was exhausted and worried that we wouldn't make it as a team. Maybe buying him was a huge and dangerous mistake. Maybe he was too much for me. Maybe I wasn't good enough.

I've had similar misgivings on a few business ventures and career moves.

It's inevitable. At some point during a reinvention, you will begin to doubt. You may doubt the path, your decisions, your approach, your offerings, the ability of your team, and even your ability to deliver your work. Little voices in your head fight between staying the course and giving up. We all experience this at times.

But when doubt consumes you, despair seeps in and darkens your perspective. You feel shaken, raw, vulnerable, and unsure of how to move forward. It brings you to tears. What you desperately crave seems elusive and not in the cards for you. It doesn't feel fair. You begin to break down.

During a "break down," you break apart. Your hopes, dreams, past experiences, jobs, skills, talents, and passions fall at your feet like leaves from a tree. They may look disparate, disorderly, and appear to make no sense. But there are many gifts in this process. It's an opportunity to see what you may not have been able to see before. It gives you a chance to reevaluate what's important and your values, your strengths, and where you want to place yourself. Common threads and themes begin to emerge from the parts of you. Gradually you reconstitute them into a new you: a stronger you, a more coherent you. And you break through. This process can be agonizing, but if you persevere, you will get through. Amazing possibilities are on the other side. That I know for sure.

In this chapter, we'll take a look at how to successfully break down to break through. I've used this approach to get myself and clients through some hard times. You'll also see how Lemon Squeezy and I reached a new understanding. Warning: this story may require you to suspend disbelief!

The "Break Down" Components: Doing and Being

I look at the verb "break down" as a process consisting of two components: doing and being. Doing involves physical actions, such as your work habits, behaviors, business services, and operations. Being is your emotional state from moment to moment. It is influenced by your beliefs, thoughts, assumptions, and values.

During the "break down" process, you scrutinize both doing and being to dissect what you're doing and why and how you're showing up. You explore where and how you're using your time and energy. As you go through this exercise, you gain insights into what must be changed to break through.

Many people underestimate the *being* and focus only on taking lots of action. But being is a powerful underlying force that you must contend with or risk sabotaging your reinvention, or any goal. As a leader, you must reconcile both components along the journey to ensure forward progress.

Let's consider how to assess the doing and being.

THE DOING

Breaking a goal down into tiny actionable pieces is my go-to approach to combat overwhelm and thoughts of "I can't do this!" If you take tiny action, you begin to gain momentum. As you begin to gain momentum, doubt begins to dissipate. Small surges of energy propel you forward and you begin to feel better. Ah, sweet relief.

But, this only works if achieving your goal is important to you and your actions align with this goal. Some action is wasteful, uses up valuable energy, and gets you nowhere. Other action may appear wasteful but is critical. Assess your action to be sure that all that you're doing is effective and will pay off.

To assess your doing, begin with a review of your goal. Your goal may be to get a new job that you love, feel more confident as a leader and better engage your team, achieve sustainable long-term growth, start a company, sell your company, successfully complete a huge project, or win a new contract, among others. These are big goals. They must be broken down into actionable steps. I use the SMART goal process to set goals and actions. SMART goals are specific (S), measurable (M), achievable (A), relevant (R), and time-bound (T).

First review your overall goal to be sure it is still a top priority. Sometimes goals shift. Then assess the specific activities: the doing. Here are a few questions to consider in your assessment.

Assess the overall goal

1. What is the goal?

2. Why is it important? The response to this question helps determine relevance and priority.

3. Does it align with your values?

4. What will be achieved by this goal? (gains, benefits)

5. What are the costs? (financial, physical, emotional)

6. What is the timeline for the goal?

7. What resources are needed?

8. What else may be affected by this?

9. What are the major milestones?

10. What would simplify this process?

11. What is the first step, second step, third step, etc. Be sure to develop bite-sized steps. This is the "achievable" part of the SMART goal. You may choke if the step is too big. Less is more.

12. Who is accountable for each step? By when?

13. What are the contingencies—what happens if I/we miss deadlines?

14. Is it worth it?

Assess the activities (your doing)

1. What are you doing?

2. Why are you doing it?

3. Does it align with your bigger vision?

4. Does it use your strengths?

5. What is gained?

6. What is the cost?

7. Is it necessary?

8. Could it be simplified? Outsourced?

9. Does it have to be done now?

10. Do you like doing it?

11. Do you want to keep doing it?

12. Is it worth it?

If you're starting to feel stuck, reconnect with your goal, your overall vision. If your goal is not meaningful enough to you, it may be time to consider pursuing something else. Be honest.

If you are committed to your goal, reignite your spark. To do so, talk with others, identify and list all that you have achieved so far, reevaluate priorities and timelines, break down your action items into smaller pieces, eliminate some action items, or take a break. Ask yourself: What is the tiniest and easiest thing I can do today to inch forward? What's the best use of my time today to advance the goal? What would give me more peace? Then go do it. You'll feel better. There are some days when "just showing up" is enough. Keep showing up for yourself and your goal.

My initial goal with Lemon Squeezy was to create a series of video-taped workshops around leadership and reinvention as he reinvented from racehorse to a fun riding partner. My goal was to have this all wrapped up within our first year together. We achieved the workshops, but I had not accounted for something critical: Lemon Squeezy Time. Lemon Squeezy Time is "whatever time it takes." You can't rush Lemon Squeezy and you certainly cannot rush building trust. This brings us to the being.

THE BEING

Not only must you take specific action toward your goal, you must also consider how you see yourself and the goal and what you believe is possible for you. How you are showing up emotionally and energetically is central to your being. During the "break down" process, emotions are high and volatile. To move forward, you must move past fear to the soul of your being. I call this your truth. Your truth can guide you if you listen. Your truth is a place of peace and knowing, but you can't find it if you're emotional.

Much suffering and stress is the result of self-judgment, comparison anxiety, and being attached to a certain outcome. Your self-worth becomes linked to performance. For example, you may think, "If I achieve the goal, I am worthy and valued. If I do not achieve the goal, I am unworthy and not valued." Or, "If I am recognized by others, I am valued; if I am ignored, I am not valued." Release these judgments and give yourself permission to be okay without them. Give your best, learn from missteps, and allow the results to manifest on their own.

To assess your being, ask yourself the following questions:

1. Who do I need to be to achieve this goal?

2. How am I showing up for myself right now?

3. What do I believe about this?

4. What am I assuming?

5. How else can I think about this?

6. What is working?

7. What do I know for sure?

8. What needs to be released?

9. Who/what must be forgiven? (including yourself)

10. What would give me more peace right now?

As you respond to these questions, notice how your emotions shift. Your emotions show you where your energy is high and positive. You can use your feelings to help guide your path.

For example, one client was promoted to senior director in a fast-growing IT firm. This was a high achievement and recognized her many years of hard work. Her supervisor and team were excited for her and hugely supportive. But within a couple of weeks of working in the new role, she suffered debilitating migraines, insomnia, and was weepy and indecisive. She felt completely out of control. After each coaching session, she resolved to overcome her challenges, be a great director, and not disappoint her team. I asked her to take a strengths assessment to identify core strengths. Research shows that people who use their top strengths in their work are happier and more productive.[13]

Following the assessment, we discovered that this new position was a terrible fit for her strengths. The stress consumed her, and she was unable to give her best. She felt constant pressure. We discussed options, including leaving the firm. But she loved the firm. Three months later, she approached her supervisor and asked for a demotion back to her former position. Her supervisor was shocked, but agreed, and within one day, all of my client's physical issues disappeared. She was happy, working in alignment with her strengths and able to give her best as she had for so many years. She had to rediscover the core of who she was, overcome her own feelings of shame, and voice her true desires. This took a lot of courage. Breaking herself down into her values and strengths, and asking for what she really wanted were key to her breakthrough.

I had a similar experience at one point in my career. I was courted by a law firm to support environmental advocacy for their clients. The CEO treated me to dinner, painted a glorious picture of his vision, and offered me a significant increase in salary. My ego jumped at the opportunity. The next day I resigned from my great job and left a team I loved. I began trekking in each day to this fancy firm. I commuted over 90 minutes each way. This stressed my personal life, took me away from the horses, and was inconsistent with my core values. In addition, the work was suspect and I was disturbed by some of the practices at the firm. In less than three months, I was miserable. I called my former supervisor. I apologized for leaving him and told him that I had made a colossal mistake. He rehired me. I was overjoyed. We worked together for many years.

The "Break Down to Break Through" Process

Once you've assessed the doing and being parts, it's time to let go of what's not working or no longer relevant, retain what works, and refocus your efforts. This sounds simple, but can be challenging. Most of us live cloaked in patterns of behavior we've used for years. We get attached to certain ways of doing things and certain ways of being. The ego likes the familiar. Familiar feels safe. When the ego feels threatened, it lashes out and resists. You may have to go slower than you prefer to maintain internal peace.

At the most fundamental level, the "break through" process frees up physical and emotional energy so that you can move forward. It consists of four steps:

1. Pause—breathe and stop what you're doing. Take a time-out.

2. Assess your doing and being.

3. Course correct. Make changes to your doing and being based on your assessment.

4. Repower and move forward.

Commit to eliminating the energy drains you found in your assessment. Be willing to see and do things differently than before. Open and adapt to a new normal, a new way of operating. This helps you repower and focus energy on what you want to achieve. The results can be impressive. Here's what a breakthrough can look like.

One client gave up her perfectionist tendencies after challenging her belief that she had to do everything herself. She embraced a new belief that hiring the right people can help you succeed. She hired an incredible team, empowered them with clear expectations, and trusted them with autonomy. She also reached out to experts in other departments of the firm to collaborate on projects. Her clients are now better served, her team is engaged and supportive, and she has more free time to do whatever she wants.

Another client's goal was to create and implement an online training program. The magnitude of the effort was taking her full focus, bogging her down, and cash flow was becoming a challenge. After considering options, she shifted her priorities. She decided to offer a series of live workshops to give her clients immediate support and generate cash flow while she sorted out the requirements for the online program. Content from the workshops was then repurposed and fed into the online program for later use. This is a great example of leveraging impact while making progress toward your goal. Just a few tweaks were required for this breakthrough.

Another client streamlined her offerings and repackaged them for higher value. That action part was easy. The tricky part was to establish the pricing. She struggled with her own sense of value and was losing money from low pricing strategies. We conducted some deep inquiry to help her discover her unique value to clients. Following this shift in beliefs, she adjusted her pricing, her clients benefited from the new offerings, and her profits skyrocketed.

Other clients have used this "break down to break through" strategy to reposition themselves in more exciting and challenging jobs with higher salaries, earning more income than they ever thought possible.

To break through, you don't have to change everything or take huge risks. Not everything has to be fixed right away. Try out new activities from the safety of the familiar. For example, if you think you may want to change careers, explore what it would be like in that new career by volunteering to do something in that industry. Attend events and get to know people. Placing yourself in a desired environment on a regular basis can open doors you never thought possible. Some passions can be nurtured as an avocation while you earn a solid salary and benefits doing something different.

You can use this same approach as a business owner to grow new opportunities. For example, volunteering as part of a nonprofit board or sponsoring a program or event can give you new contacts and business relationships that could be mutually beneficial. Just be sure that you have a sincere interest in the organization. Do not volunteer if you are not committed to the cause. Your activity will become an energy drain if it is not aligned with your values.

Make tiny changes and notice what happens. It could be as simple as taking a breath to settle and noticing how your body begins to relax. When Lemon Squeezy exhales deeply, he begins to relax. That breath is evidence of relaxation and a willingness to accept and learn. Both are central to progressing as a team. What are you noticing? What you focus on expands.

A note of caution: although you have assessed your doing and being and made changes, you may not see immediate results. Many folks get frustrated with a perceived lack of "progress" at this point. High achievers are used to making tangible, steady, fast progress toward their goals. In my experience, patience is not always their best strength, especially if they cannot see evidence.

Much progress is invisible. You can't see it or feel it, but it's happening. Have faith and work your new approach every day. Be consistent and committed. The physical results will follow. Breakthroughs run on "Lemon Squeezy Time," which is highly unpredictable. A breakthrough may be painfully slow or happen in an instant. Be persistent. Show up for yourself.

A Break Down to Break Through with Lemon Squeezy

I had to use the "break down to break through" process with Lemon Squeezy several times to get my doing and being in order. The "doing" wasn't as effective as I had hoped. My "being" also needed some shifts. Here's what happened.

We had been working together for a few months, and his training was progressing. But, one big piece was still missing: trust. He did not feel safe. He looked for danger everywhere. The slightest sound, movement of a tree branch or squirrel would set him off running. He even spooked in the barn with the other horses present and at his hay piles outside. Overall, he felt unsafe and did not see me as his leader. In fact, at times he didn't see me at all. This was surprising, since he wasn't that way when I first tried him out. But, horse behavior can change in different environments, and it was a cold and blustery winter.

I upped my training, learned new techniques, and the vet, chiropractor, and saddle fitter examined him. He checked out fine physically, but nothing seemed to fully ease his mental tension. Experts told me that it just takes time. But it didn't get much better. I couldn't trot one full lap around the ring without him darting off. Even though we'd recover from the spooks, it was not the safe and fun partnership I desired.

I began to question my leadership effectiveness and training abilities. I blamed myself for causing him anxiety. This quickly spiraled into self-doubt, the killer of all progress. On our darkest day, he spooked while I was leading him and almost ran me over again, despite consistent lessons on boundaries which I thought he had learned. It was the tipping point. I burst into tears. "I can't do this," I said. "I've made a huge mistake. Who am I to think that I would be good enough to work with you. That's it, I'm moving you on." I led him back to the barn, took off his tack, and turned him out. I sobbed in the barn, feeling guilty and so disappointed in myself. I felt like I had failed us both. I felt like I had failed the mission. I wasn't up to the task.

The next day I traveled to attend a weekend lecture while continuing to stew in my shortcomings. At a lunch break, I shared my issues about Lemon Squeezy with a friend. She listened and then said, "I feel that he just doesn't understand his job. Maybe you should talk with him." She's an intuitive and can connect with animals. It was true that I had never really explained to him what his job could be. Perhaps he saw all these training activities as disparate meaningless parts with no purpose. I've had some jobs like that. It feels terrible when you're uninformed of the larger vision and how your specific role contributes. It's unclear and scary. Everyone needs clarity. With clarity comes confidence. I teach that. I gave this some thought over the weekend.

I decided I would "talk" to Lemon Squeezy. I have taken animal communication classes in the past, but I'm not great at reading my own animals. It was worth a try. I had nothing to lose. Here's how it went down.

I sat in the bedroom; he was in his stall. I settled my mind, imagined a connection between our hearts, and began to send him images of everything he's done well. I felt nothing from him, but I continued anyway. I explained that those activities are all part of a bigger goal to do other things together like cantering across fields, jumping small fences, doing dressage, and trail riding. I pictured those activities. I told him that we need to learn certain things before we can do those other things. Then I paused. Still nothing. I waited a few moments.

Suddenly a question emerged. "Can we do those other things now?" Something was happening. I felt him listening. I answered, "We could probably do them now, but I don't feel safe doing them until our basics are more firm and you're not so jumpy." I told him that I'd always do my best to keep him safe and that his job is to keep me safe too. I asked him if he wanted to do the activities I envisioned together and told him that it was okay if he didn't. I would find him a new owner if he wanted. I paused and waited. A lump began to form in my throat as I fought back tears. After a long pause, I heard, "I'll get back to you." He needed to think about it. His answer made me smile, since it seemed like something he would say. He's a very deliberate horse and this was a very serious question. I said "sure" and suggested that he also talk with the other horses. He could get back to me when he was ready.

The next morning I walked out to the barn to bring in the horses for feeding. Lemon Squeezy stood in the back of his field huddled with his buddies Frescoe and Noble. I swear it looked like they were holding a meeting. I picked up a halter to catch Lemon Squeezy. He was locked in conversation with Frescoe and Noble, their noses touching. I called his name. He looked up, spun around, and cantered to me. He had never done that before. Normally he saunters over and takes his time. He seemed happy to see me. Frescoe and Noble stayed put. That is also unusual. At feeding time, if one horse comes running, the others usually follow. I stroked Lemon Squeezy's face and told him how much I appreciated him. He made a sweet face and put his head in the halter. I felt that he had said yes to continuing our work together. That day we had an amazing ride, a breakthrough. It was a new beginning for our partnership.

Chapter 9

Five Key Tactics for Growth

Growth is an ongoing pursuit for business owners, leaders, and anyone looking to give their best. As you go through the reinvention process, you grow. A successful reinvention requires desire, intention, and discipline to show up and continue to take action. Below is a list of the top five growth tactics I use for myself, with clients, and also with my horses.

1. Lighten your load.

2. Take baby steps to expand your comfort zone.

3. Use the power of the opposite to open new thinking.

4. Set boundaries and rules of engagement.

5. Acknowledge the "try" and savor small wins.

Let's consider each one, and I'll share how I use them in Lemon Squeezy's reinvention.

Lighten Your Load

Every day you carry a load of responsibilities and emotions. Some days the load feels heavy. Other days it feels light. When you're reinventing, your load increases as you plan and build something new. In the beginning, excitement propels you forward. But over time, the increased load may feel burdensome and almost too much to bear. Past emotions may come back to haunt you, testing you with doubt. Your load may begin to squash you. It can feel difficult to move.

To avoid carrying too much, check in with your load. Ask yourself the following questions:

1. What am I carrying?

2. How does it feel?

3. Is it mine?

4. Is it necessary?

5. Who can help lighten it?

Many of us take on the responsibilities of others, worry about the future, and hold on to past anxieties. This can bog you down.

For example, one of my clients worked full-time as a corporate vice president, served on multiple boards of directors, and played a key role in several volunteer efforts, all while raising a family. Her brilliance and skills were in top demand. Because she could do the work and has a big heart, she said yes to most requests. But she was exhausted and stressed. She felt guilty all the time—she wasn't spending much time with her family and she was unable to give her best to all commitments. She carried a heavy load. Just because you can do the tasks doesn't mean you have to or should.

She began to challenge her beliefs about her duties to society. She reduced her commitments and focused on a few priority areas. As a result, she felt happier and more productive. She was able to focus on what she most loved.

To lighten your load, reassign work, accept a smaller piece of a project, or say no to new engagements. If you're hanging on to a limiting belief or emotion, let it go. This provides immediate relief and frees you to move forward. One of my clients let go of a lifetime of guilt trying to be everything to everyone. Releasing that heavy burden ushered in a new sense of peace and calm.

Horses carry loads too. I have to pay close attention to how they feel about carrying their load. A few horses from my past decided I was not the load they wanted to carry—one good "buck" tossed me right off!

My horse Frescoe enjoys the load he carries. We've been together from his birth. Ever since the first day I sat on his back, he has carried me with respect and pride. It's almost as if he says, "Look what I get to carry!" He also chooses what he wants to carry—sometimes he prefers not to do equine-assisted learning work with groups. I listen and use another horse.

When I first started working with Lemon Squeezy, he carried a high worry load. He was always on the lookout for danger. As a herd animal, that's a valuable skill to ensure safety, but not when we're riding. His worry took up valuable brain space that we needed for our training. It caused distraction and an inability to focus on his work. He didn't yet trust me as his leader to ensure that the environment was safe.

How many of us worry about things that are not our responsibility? Let that go and focus on what's yours. Carry your own load and let others carry theirs.

If your load is too heavy, empower others to help. Surround yourself with team members with required specific expertise. Know their strengths and be sure they get to use them. This creates a sense of ownership and engagement, deepens connection and commitment, and builds relationships for the long term. It creates a culture of accountability where all willingly carry their own load. It also distributes the load and takes the pressure off of you to do everything.

Let others help you. Hire experts to help in areas where you or your team lack experience. I have a team of experts who help me with the horses—traditional veterinarians, holistic veterinarians, an osteopath, chiropractors, acupuncturist, farrier, barn cleaning support, and trusted trainers. I also have a team that helps me with my business.

I have a very special team that helps me train Lemon Squeezy: my horses Frescoe and Noble. Frescoe is my retired riding partner. He's a wise and benevolent soul. Noble is a highly sensitive and athletic horse. He was born on our farm and has taught me a lot about riding with lightness and specificity. He is masterful at "sideways stuff," anything that involves lateral movement.

Before a session with Lemon Squeezy, I talk to Frescoe and Noble in their stalls. That may sound crazy, but I believe animals talk to each other and know way more than humans would ever expect.

I asked Frescoe to help Lemon Squeezy with his confidence; I asked Noble to help him understand leg yield, a basic sideways move. Did they listen? Read on.

Each time I requested specific help, Lemon Squeezy was more calm and more confident in his riding sessions. He spooked less and his leg yield improved. It was astounding. Following these sessions, Frescoe checked in with me. He nickered as we entered the barn and looked me straight in the eye, as if asking how it went. He never did that before I began soliciting his input. As soon as I gave him feedback on the session, he averted his eyes and resumed eating hay. I thank Frescoe and Noble each time. I am grateful for their help.

Engaging Frescoe and Noble in their strengths gave both horses a sense of purpose and appreciation of their value. I believe they enjoyed carrying that part of the load.

When your load is lightened, you can move forward with ease.

Expand Your Comfort Zone—Take Baby Steps

No growth is possible without moving outside of your comfort zone. Your comfort zone is where you feel safe and know what to expect. Your confidence is high.

Just outside of your comfort zone is your stretch zone. This is where you feel less comfortable and less safe. You are not sure what to expect. The stretch zone is where new learning occurs. I've found small regular doses of "stretch" work best to expand your comfort zone.

Beyond the stretch zone is the fear zone. You feel unsafe and scared in this zone. Every cell in your body screams for you to run back to the familiar. I believe that stepping a toe into the fear zone on a regular basis promotes growth. But tread lightly. Don't scare yourself so much that you never step out again!

Expanding your comfort zone is like learning to swim. I taught my brother to swim when he was six. He loved the water, but was terrified of swimming. We spent many hours splashing along the side of the pool while hanging on to the wall. We played games like "how fast can you kick" and blew bubbles underwater. I held his hands as he kicked with vigor and propelled me around the pool. One day he was ready. He released my hands and swam to me in two strokes. I'll never forget his face—shocked, laughing, and eager for more. It seemed to happen in an instant. It didn't. He had expanded his comfort zone by working in his stretch zone. He explored and took risks while having fun. A whole new world opened.

During reinvention, you expand your comfort zone. You live in the stretch zone and dabble at the edge of the fear zone. You may feel scared and excited at the same time.

The best way to expand your comfort zone is through baby steps. Each day ask yourself, "What is the smallest step I can take today to advance my goal?" It may be connecting with an industry leader, talking with a colleague, attending an event, posting an article on social media, or compiling a list of prospects. Taking one or more baby steps each day adds up and yields powerful results over time.

For example, a financially struggling business owner may "suddenly" get a great new client that propels the company into financial abundance. A senior executive may "suddenly" receive an invitation to join an exciting fast-growing firm. Other opportunities may "suddenly" open for you, such as key board of director positions, new inspiring group initiatives, speaking events, media interviews that raise your profile, or introductions to key industry players who can open new doors. Many of my clients have experienced this type of growth. I have too. But there is really nothing "sudden" about it. All of these opportunities are the result of consistent action and showing up. They are the result of many hours of baby steps preparing, planting seeds, and sowing the ground outside of your comfort zone. It is an intentional process.

Stepping out of your comfort zone requires you to take risks, be seen and heard, and grow your skills. For me, this involved public speaking.

When I was younger and worked in engineering, public speaking scared me. My heart raced, my palms sweat, and my body heated up like a fiery inferno. I suffered through meetings and presentations and felt like a flustered mess.

I decided that I needed to be a solid public speaker. I started by taking baby steps. I organized monthly luncheons to allow technical experts to share about their projects. As the organizer, I introduced the speaker and topic each month. It was a simple and easy way to start. It became fun, and I started to see the value of creating a comfortable learning environment. I set my ego aside and taught myself to focus on the topic and its utility to the audience. Over time, these luncheons gave me confidence.

When I launched my current business, I offered to speak at every venue I could to help business leaders grow. I was a bit nervous, but

I knew the information would be valuable to others. This led to more opportunities and to more clients.

Now I love public speaking and do it professionally. It's a great way to leverage impact since many people benefit at once. But I had to expand my comfort zone to make this happen. If I hadn't, I would have denied myself this powerful tool to help others.

Growth doesn't stop, and there is always a new test for your comfort zone. My Reinvention in the Round program with Lemon Squeezy challenged my growth edge again. The program blended public speaking with video in front of a live audience with a horse I barely knew. The first session was scheduled for the dead of winter. The videos would be posted on YouTube for all to see. What could go wrong?

The possibilities for this program both excited and terrified me. I decided that the potential learning experience for clients outweighed all my insecurities. It did. Many called the program "life-changing."

I used baby steps with Lemon Squeezy to help him to gain confidence with me, our farm, and the training program. For our first three months, our training sessions were never more than 10–20 minutes. I never forced him to do anything. I worked with him every day to build trust. Some days I stood with him as he grazed. Other days I led him as close to the cow field as he felt comfortable. He was scared of cows. Many days I worked with him with only a halter and lead rope. I had to learn his comfort zone, stretch zone, and fear zone. Each day was different. The same is true with people.

If you're leading others through change, know when you're asking someone to step outside of their comfort zone. Understand how far out this request may be for them. Allow them to take baby steps. As a trusted leader, it's your responsibility to grow your team's abilities while keeping them safe. If you make them feel too unsafe, you may lose their trust and their willingness to stick around.

93

A positive outcome is the result of many baby steps. Each baby step on its own may seem quite insignificant, and you may not even notice any result. That's okay. Keep going.

The Power of the Opposite

We tend to be creatures of habit. We like routine and knowing what to expect. That gives us comfort. But it can also cause us to go on autopilot and limit creative thought. That is not good for reinvention. I once asked someone how he was doing. He said, "Same stuff, different day." He was stuck in a rut. His patterns held him captive.

Exercises that encourage you to do the opposite of what you would normally do (as long as they are safe!) break these patterns and allow your brain to search for new possibilities. Doing the opposite encourages you to be present, aware, and deliberate. It helps you to slow down and focus. It inspires new insights. It can also be great fun. Joy and humor are wonderful ways to relax and stimulate new thinking.

To prompt new thinking, try these exercises:

1. Question storming—Instead of a brainstorming session, consider holding a session in which only questions are allowed. For example, frame all questions using the "Who, What, Why, When, How, and What If" format. Making your brain search for questions shifts how you examine an issue and inspires creativity.

2. Walk backwards, stand instead of sit, stand on one leg, write with your nondominant hand. Moving your body in a way that is unexpected upsets patterns and causes you to focus and pay attention. For example, a friend and I were sitting together discussing a new

name for her offering. We were struggling, so I decided to stand on one leg. Within 20 seconds I came up with several compelling names. She was shocked, amused, and grateful.

3. Less is more—How quiet can you be? Whisper or use no voice. Quiet and subtle communication and action makes others pay close attention. Or, instead of taking more action at work, do nothing, meditate, or take a walk.

4. React with curiosity and empathy—Instead of anger or criticism, get curious or show empathy when things go wrong. Providing an unexpected emotional response challenges a patterned behavior and opens an opportunity for new understanding.

5. Identify the "gift"—There are lessons and gifts in every experience. Find something wonderful to acknowledge. For example, losing a big client is painful at first, but opens the door to shifting your business model and supporting new and better clients.

USING THE OPPOSITE WITH LEMON SQUEEZY

I use the opposite approach with horses to get them engaged. Horses love routine. They feel safe when they follow an expected pattern and a consistent leader. But sometimes they check out and go on autopilot. They stop listening and react without thinking. They become the human equivalent of "asleep at work." Lemon Squeezy was not asleep. But he was not engaged. We had other issues.

When Lemon Squeezy first came to our farm, leading him from his stall to the pasture was treacherous. The jostling of horse blankets hanging on the stall doors caused him to spin and try to bolt down the barn aisle. He charged the horse in the stall next to him and pinned back his ears at every passerby. Going in and out of his pasture gate was dangerous. He'd spin around and take off as I was closing the gate, nearly slamming me in the head. In this environment, he did not yet feel safe.

One of the first things I did was address his dangerous behavior at the pasture gate. Dodging a leaping horse was not what I wanted to deal with every day. I surveyed the situation to see what could help. Ah, grass. Grass in the middle of winter is a rare treat, and I had noticed that he was food motivated. I haltered him, opened the gate, and invited him to graze the grass just outside the gate. This was the opposite of what he expected. At first he looked around with suspicion, certain something would jump out. But the grass was too tempting. He spent some time grazing, and then I put him back in his field. This was the start of breaking up that behavior and creating a new possibility.

We practiced that approach for the next few days, and it worked. He was calm and quiet walking in and out of his field. He didn't even grab for grass. He was very respectful and enjoyed grass when I let him.

We also used the opposite for mounting. Once I climbed aboard, I asked him to stand still. As an ex-racehorse, this was a challenge. He expected me to jump aboard and off we'd go. I'm sure he thought I was the slowest human on earth. It took some patience, but he figured it out.

Using the opposite approach, Lemon Squeezy learned to chase birds in the indoor arena instead of running from them. As a bird flew over, I encouraged him to trot after it. Once he realized that he could move the birds instead of them spooking him, he trotted after them with confidence and power. I used this technique years ago when my first horse Dixie was freaked out by a plastic sandwich bag blowing in the wind. We chased that sandwich bag all over the arena. She stomped the bag with her hoof when it landed. She "killed" it. I've never seen a more proud horse. In jumping competitions, I'd tell her to "kill the baggie" when she felt nervous at a big fence, and she'd fly right over.

Set Boundaries and Rules of Engagement

As you move through the reinvention process, it's important to set up boundaries and rules of engagement. A structure lets you and others know what to expect. This protects your time and energy and allows you to focus on top priorities. When you take charge of your time and energy, you feel fantastic.

Think about how you work best. Here are a few questions to consider:

1. What are your work hours?

2. How many appointments can you take in a day?

3. When are you available for meetings?

4. Can you work at home? What are the expectations if you work from home?

5. Is weekend work expected? If so, will it be compensated?

6. How often will you have team meetings?

7. What kinds of issues should be elevated and who has authority for what?

8. Who can make decisions in your absence?

9. When is your downtime?

10. What does self-care look like and how much time is required?

Be sure to mark your downtime and self-care time on your calendar to be sure you do it. Treat it like any other appointment. Honor it and show up. This will serve you well long-term.

Here are some examples of rules of engagement from my clients. Notice the range. Your rules of engagement may be very different. Create ones that work best for you, your team, and your clients.

Example Rules of Engagement

- Meetings are by appointment only.
- Every meeting must have an agenda which can be addressed in one hour or less.
- Schedule meetings only in the afternoons. Mornings are for writing, researching.
- Never attend evening networking events. Evening is for family.
- Never attend luncheon networking meetings; the workday is for work.
- Attend no more than two evening networking events per month.
- No appointments on Fridays.
- Check email only upon start of work and fifteen minutes before the end of the workday.
- Respond to all emails within 24 hours.
- Three days a week in office from 11:00 am–8:00 pm; other days 9:00 am–5:00 pm
- Serve on no more than three boards at once.
- Serve on only one board per year.
- One hour of meditation and journaling every day.
- Three one-hour workouts a week during lunch break scheduled in 90-minute blocks.
- Daily 30-minute workouts before work.
- Volunteer at one nonprofit organization/year.
- Conduct one pro bono effort/year.
- Say three gratitudes and three affirmations before bedtime.
- Schedule worry time.

Here are my rules of engagement for Lemon Squeezy:

- Stay out of my physical space unless you're invited.
- Nasty face does not get treats.
- Stand quietly for grooming and saddling, and you will get treats.
- Stand quietly for mounting, and you will get a treat.
- Do not bite me in the butt no matter how tempting it is.
- Our training sessions are less than an hour.
- Full presence is desired; pay attention.
- Feel the fear, let it go, and get on with your greatness.

Acknowledge the "Try" and Savor Small Wins

As you go through the reinvention process, you may feel that you're not making any progress. Tangible evidence of success may not yet be visible. That's normal. Seeds take time to sprout. In the meantime, focus on the striving, the action that you are taking toward your goals. Acknowledge the "try." As hockey great Wayne Gretzky said, "You miss 100% of the shots you never take." Notice your shots. Savor each attempt, and learn from it.

Look for "progress, not perfection," some smart person said a long time ago. This advice is used in 12-step treatment programs and for a variety of efforts, including dieting, improving physical fitness, and in horse training. It's great advice for reinvention.

Progress shows up in different ways and can be quite subtle. For example, as I work with Lemon Squeezy, I may notice a small shift in his eye from tension to relaxation, or one of his ears pointed in my direction. Both of these responses indicate that he notices me. As I put his halter on, he dips his head lower, making it easier to attach the halter. These behaviors give me great joy, since they indicate progress and a willingness to see me and to work with me.

I also notice how he breathes. When I mount up to ride, I notice if he exhales or holds his breath. If he exhales, he relaxes. I savor that. If he does not exhale, I notice and think about how I can help him relax more before I get on.

Noticing your own "tries" and the tries of others lets you appreciate small wins along your path. It helps to build morale and momentum. Notice your own commitment and that of others. Notice when you choose to respond with calm to a frustrating situation. Notice your own moments of peace and deep exhales. Savor them.

Not noticing or acknowledging the efforts of others is a big problem in the work world. One of the most common complaints I hear from senior leaders and executives is that they feel they are taken for granted. They do not feel appreciated at work or for volunteer efforts. Sometimes this results in a resignation.

Feeling appreciated is key to success. Notice and acknowledge specific contributions and efforts. Show your appreciation. Recognize individual and team efforts. One thank-you note or email can make someone's day.

You can formalize noticing the "try" by creating success metrics. In business, we use key performance indicators (KPIs) to track progress toward goals. You can create KPIs for anything. Consider what success would look like along the way to your goals. Develop KPIs based on the activities required to meet your goals. Break those activities down into smaller actions.

For example, let's say you are opening a new consulting business and you would like to raise awareness of your expertise. Based on your strengths, you believe that the best way to do that is through speaking and writing.

The activities involved in raising awareness could include the following:

1. Writing and publishing a blog once a week

2. Attending one networking event/week

3. Giving one talk/month

4. Meeting with industry leaders once a week

5. Serving on a nonprofit board of directors

Based on these activities, your KPIs could be:

- Number of blogs published/month
- Number of networking events attended/month
- Number of speaking events/month
- Number of meetings/month with key prospects and industry leaders
- Number of thank-you notes or emails sent/month

To savor the "try," break these activities down further. For example, if you're busy one day and only have time to jot down three main bullets or a short outline for your blog, acknowledge that action. Registering for a networking event or conference shows your intention. Acknowledge that action. Reaching out via phone or email to new prospects and industry leaders is the first action step toward securing a meeting or board position. Acknowledge the outreach.

As you track your activities, notice what is working best to deepen relationships, expand your reach, and close deals. Be sure your topics are important to your target market and that you are positioning your articles and talks in front of the right audience. Learn from the responses to your articles, talks, and meetings. Make changes to your content or approach based on the responses. As you better address your market needs, you will gain more visibility and respect. This will help you increase sales.

Knowing your conversion rate—for example, the number of meetings it takes to make one sale or the number of sales gained per talk—is important. But, if you only focus on the number of sales each month, you miss acknowledging and learning from your efforts. If the number of sales each month is low, you may become discouraged and quit. Noticing, savoring, and learning from your "tries" gives you a more comprehensive picture of what you are building. Relationships take time. The depth of relationships is difficult to measure. But if you consistently show up with helpful information in front of the right people, you will get work.

I use KPIs to track progress with Lemon Squeezy. In 2018, we logged 205 training sessions, including 99 rides. The numbers represent my commitment to show up. The comments on the sessions provide qualitative feedback on how I'm showing up, his response, and on our relationship. The comments range from "relaxed, peaceful, nice bend, great halt, soft flexion, both eyes," to "wild, tense, stiff, spooky, no left bend, leaning right shoulder, cow snort, no eye." Progress is not linear. The qualitative details acknowledge the "tries" and allow me to step back and see patterns of what is working and what needs to be adjusted. This is important for any reinvention. (By the way, "cow snort" is an alarm just before he bolts off. Cow snort is not desired. I hope you do not have a cow snort during your reinvention.)

What "tries" will you notice and savor? What KPIs work best for you? Next, let's explore how to keep going for long-term success.

Chapter 10

Resilience for Sustainable Success

Navigating change requires resilience and good emotional and physical balance. Resilience is the ability to bounce back from challenges and stay the course to your goal. Balance is a dynamic state, not something you achieve once and check off your list. Like a gymnast on a balance beam, you must make constant micro-corrections to stay upright. This takes awareness and practice.

Stress is a mighty foe and can run high during a reinvention. It sneaks up on you, making you tolerate more and more. If you are not resilient, stress may cause burnout, physical illness, decreased productivity, or loss of profits. You may crash. It's important to build restorative practices into your daily routine for long-term success.

In this chapter, we'll discuss resilience practices to foster sustainable well-being. The goal is to find activities that you will commit to do on a regular basis. Calendaring these activities helps you create a customized resilience plan. Following your plan will allow you to thrive. I learned resilience the hard way. I didn't bounce. In this chapter, I'll share the story.

Nature and Productivity

Nature gives us great examples of how to be resilient. Tree limbs bend in the wind. Tree roots grow deep into the earth for nourishment and support. I spend a lot of time sitting by our wetland observing nature. Wetlands are some of the most biologically diverse and productive ecosystems on earth. But in winter, wetlands look like dead zones. The brown grasses lay flat. Hues of beige cover the land. Dry stemmy stalks wait for spring.

High productivity is not a constant state in nature. Even the most productive systems need to rest. Dormancy conserves energy and is essential to a productive spring.

But humans tend to keep pushing. We punish ourselves for not being "productive enough." We compare ourselves to others and to our own previous success. We expect to always do "better." Nature knows the truth. We must rest and recharge to grow.

For years, I didn't understand this. I strived for more production. I buried myself in my to-do list, stressed about money, and drove myself to exhaustion to get things done and prove my worth. I was sure that if I relaxed and let down my guard, something would fail. I worried that I would lose everything and be exposed as a fraud. It was a crummy way to live and challenged my peace of mind. It also ran me down physically. Can you relate? It took me many years to release that pattern and embrace what nature showed me every day. But when I did, a whole new world opened. I finally felt free, happy, healthy, and confident. I was also able to bounce back from adversity.

There are many ways to build resilience. I've found that an integrated daily practice works best. It consists of several activities that cleanse your mind, body, and soul and set you up for success. A resilience practice may not prevent you from hitting a low patch, but it will help soften the intensity and duration of the low. At a minimum, it will help you keep on going. Let's look at this integrated approach.

An Integrated Approach to Resilience—Four Key Areas

Many of the world's greatest ancient civilizations, like the ancient Egyptians, Mesopotamians, Indians, South Americans, Arabs, Native Americans, and Chinese identify four main areas required for well-being: mental, emotional, physical, and spiritual (MEPS).[14] MEPS are defined as follows:

- Mental: your thoughts, beliefs, and perspective.
- Emotional: your emotions and feelings.
- Physical: your physical body and material world.
- Spiritual: your connection to the nonmaterial world; e.g., religious or metaphysical.

Bringing awareness to these areas helps you identify what needs to shift to rebalance toward a healthier state of being. Awareness helps you listen to yourself so that you're a good partner for your own well-being. The better partner that you are for yourself, the better partner and leader you can be for others. Many of us have this backwards—we put ourselves last. That is not a sustainable approach for well-being. Now is the time to stop that practice!

By conducting activities that touch each of these areas, you increase well-being and resilience. Let's explore the MEPS, and then we'll consider specific activities for your resilience plan.

MENTAL

Your thoughts, beliefs, and perspective shape your mindset. Top athletes, performers, and business leaders know that a healthy mindset is key to success. A healthy mindset recognizes and pursues opportunities, quickly bounces back from the inevitable challenges of life and business, and keeps you on track to your goals. It fuels your actions with positivity, possibility, and power and is critical to achieving the impact you desire.

I believe that an intentionally crafted mindset is your most important asset. A less than stellar mindset steals your joy, creates worry, and yields inconsistent results. Here are five qualities of a healthy mindset.

1. Gives full attention.

2. Judgment-free.

3. Able to focus.

4. Challenges negative thoughts.

5. Forgives.

Check in with your thoughts and beliefs. If you are distracted or holding on to negativity, ask yourself, "What am I assuming? What do I believe to be true? How else can I think about this?" As you uncover these thoughts and beliefs, you empower yourself to choose different ones.

EMOTIONAL

How you feel is directly related to your mental, physical, and spiritual states. Checking in with your feelings and emotions provides insight into what shifts you may want to make to feel better. Ask yourself, "How do I feel?" several times throughout the day. For example, if you respond,

"Tired," you may need to make some adjustments to your schedule to get more rest. If you answer, "Angry," you may need to practice forgiveness or empathy. If you do not check in with your feelings, you risk missing warning signs. Exhaustion or anger can lead to overwhelm, which can lead to reduced work performance and illness. Your relationships may suffer.

Before you take on your next task or go to a meeting, pause and notice how you feel. Are you tired, stressed, fine, energetic, happy, calm, or nervous? Acknowledge your feeling. Then take a breath, let it go, and refocus your full attention on the work at hand. Be your own cheerleader. I call myself "Bessie." If I'm struggling, I tell myself, "Come on, Bessie. You've got this. Only five more minutes and you're done." The silliness makes me smile and helps me finish up whatever it is I'm doing.

PHYSICAL

Your physical body carries you through the world. Check in with your physical body every day and give it what it needs. A feeling of tension or exhaustion may be due to a lack of rest, water, movement, or good food. Nourish yourself. I've had clients who get so busy that they forget to eat, drink, or take a bathroom break. Set a timer and give yourself a break. Honor your needs. This is the only physical body you have.

The physical area also includes other people, your job, clients, your environment, home, nature, animals, and the material things that surround you. Be sure they align with your values. Work to remove anything that does not. This includes toxic people.

Check in with your physical world and appreciate its beauty. Notice what you love.

SPIRITUAL

The spiritual area gives deeper meaning to your life and can include religion, Source, Spirit, the universe, nature, or any practice that you hold sacred. It can be reached through prayer, meditation, reflection, a walk in nature, and many other ways. A spiritual connection helps you move beyond self to something bigger. It is highly personal and varies greatly between people.

Resilience Activities

There are a variety of activities that may be included under each of the MEPS. Below is a partial list of sample activities. Several activities hit more than one of the MEPS areas. For example, social time may include physical activity with friends (such as yoga or a hike), followed by a nutritious lunch with those friends. In that case, you would be addressing the physical, emotional (feeling happy and connected with friends), mental (positive mindset), and even spiritual, if yoga and/or hiking give you a sense of deeper meaning.

To create your resilience plan, pick activities that work best for you and integrate them into a regular routine. Be sure that you have at least one under each of the four MEPS. Select some activities that you can do daily and others that you can do weekly or at least monthly. I use a combination of activities on a daily basis.

For example, every day I state gratitudes, affirmations, write in my journal, and walk in nature. Most days I also work out and try to eat well. I have lunch once a week with friends and enjoy my family on weekends. My goal is to meditate at least three times per week. Sometimes I eat brownies and ice cream and cheeseburgers. As we learned in the last chapter, this is about progress, not perfection!

Experiment with different activities and schedules until you find a blend that works for you. Some people dislike meditation, but love sitting in nature. Others see journaling as a chore, but love meditating. This is your resilience plan; customize it for your needs.

Here's a partial list of activities that promote resilience:

- Gratitude—say at least three things you are grateful for each day
- Affirmations—state three affirmations (as we discussed in chapter 4)
- Set intention
- Positive mindset—what am I assuming; how else can I think about that?
- Forgiveness—self and others
- Journal
- Physical exercise
- Eat nourishing food and drink plenty of fresh water
- Sleep and rest
- Laughing
- Social time
- Meditation
- Prayer
- Reflection
- Walking in nature

Your resilience plan may not feel like it's doing anything at first. It can take some time before you begin to feel or see any results. Have faith. Stick to it. It is working beneath the surface. You're building a stronger foundation. It took me a while to rebuild my foundation after a wreck. Here's the story.

My Story

Late in 2001, we closed the division of my family's technical staffing firm that I was running. I recommended this move based on the turbulent and unsustainable market. Many clients had filed for bankruptcy. I felt the market volatility was too risky to try to ride out. We struggled to collect payments due and I was losing faith. After several painful conversations with my parents, we shut the doors.

I had no job and nothing lined up, but I had saved money to carry me for a few months. I wasn't sure what I wanted to do. For the first time in my life, I was giving myself some time to figure that out.

It was liberating and terrifying. I dabbled as a volunteer in community planning and helped develop our town's comprehensive land use plan. I trail-rode my horses and explored career options.

During this time, one of my horses sustained a ligament injury that required complete stall rest. After three months, she was ready to begin an exercise plan that involved walking outside. As she became stronger, we worked up to trotting. This was a standard protocol that I had been through before with other horses.

One cold morning in February, I tacked her up and we set off down the driveway. A few minutes into our ride, I noticed a tractor carrying a huge round bale of hay up the mountain across the street. Suddenly the round bale shook loose and tumbled down the mountain. My horse spooked, spun, and bolted across the field. Before I could stop her, the bed of a dump truck rose up at a neighboring farm. The truck bed surprised us both, but what happened next was worse. The bed was filled with gravel. As the gravel crashed to the ground, my already bolting horse started to buck. After two vigorous leaps, she tossed me. I was headed down.

I crashed to the ground with a thud, landing on my right knee. Instant nausea consumed me. I knew that I would soon pass out. I shifted my body so my right leg was on top, tilted my head so vomit would not suffocate me, and told myself to breathe. I couldn't move. I laid there for several minutes. Then I heard the "putt, putt, putt" of a tractor engine coming closer and closer. The kind elderly farmer stepped off and gazed down into my face. "Do you need some help?" he asked.

After what seemed to be an eternity, emergency vehicles streamed down our road and parked in the grass. It felt like the entire neighborhood had assembled. They heaved me into the ambulance and we raced off.

I had broken my femur in two places. After draining out the bone marrow, the surgeon inserted a titanium rod in my femur. Two screws in my knee held the rod in place. Following surgery, I felt excruciating pain between morphine drip moments. After a couple of days, I became feverish. The doctors were concerned that I might need a blood transfusion. I had severe pain in my lower leg and thought they had missed another fracture. My leg was red, hot, and swollen. An ultrasound showed two blood clots behind my knee; deep vein thrombosis, they called it. I ended up on blood thinner for five years.

After nine days in the hospital, they sent me home in the ambulance since I was still flat and couldn't sit up. Two men carried me into the house on a stretcher and laid me on my bed. I was on bed rest for two more weeks, including a bed pan, which was totally demoralizing. Nurses came to check bandages, my blood, and my general condition. It was quite humbling, but I was very grateful for all the support from my husband and family. I had never felt more vulnerable. My husband rigged up a mirror so I could watch the horses out the window while lying in bed. That gave me some relief.

The timing of the accident smacked me at my most vulnerable and triggered my deepest fears. I didn't have a job and couldn't work. Money was dwindling. I feared we would lose everything. In the past, I could always rely on my ability to work to get me through anything. But I couldn't even sit at a desk.

I felt like a wreck. The business had failed, my physical health was a mess, I wasn't sure about the future, and my young horses were getting feral. One doctor told me to never ride a horse again. "That's not happening," I replied. He said, "Then you better never fall off." Those words haunted me for years.

I progressed from a walker to a cane, and after six months, I felt a lot better. I still couldn't sit at a desk for long periods, but I could drive, and that was critical. I reached out to my network in environmental engineering. Luck was with me. One of my former colleagues was moving on to a new position. The firm needed a manager to lead her project. I applied and was overjoyed when an offer was extended. That may have been one of the luckiest moments in my life. It was a fantastic job with great people and interesting work. I started working part-time. I ended up staying for nine years. I was rebuilding.

Although I was healing physically, the emotional and psychological toll of the accident was intense. I was not the same person. I experienced sudden onsets of massive fear for no apparent reason. This would happen when I was riding my quiet horse Cali out on the trail. My body was on high alert for danger, and the fear was almost paralyzing. I also had a couple of young horses—Lila was nearly three and her sister, Coral, was a two-year-old. I found myself protective of my body even while leading them; young horses are athletic and leap about. I didn't trust that my body could move fast enough to get out of the way. I sent them off to trainers.

I worked aggressively on my fitness. By the anniversary of the accident, I achieved my goal of running three miles in 30 minutes. I know that's not extraordinary, but for me it was great. But despite being fairly fit, my brain still didn't think I was safe. This wreaked havoc on my relationships with my younger horses and even the more experienced Cali. My directions to the horses were incongruent with the fear I was feeling deep inside. It was kind of like driving a car with the brake on. "Go, but oh please don't go!" Horses hate that. So do people.

I felt that the accident was punishment for taking a break and being irresponsible about working. Maybe I didn't deserve to enjoy the farm and our horses. Maybe I didn't deserve to be happy. My fear was not about riding; my fear was that I couldn't trust myself to be a safe place for me. I had made bad decisions with terrible consequences. My thoughts traveled into dark places.

It took me seven years to work through the fear. During that time, I learned about the MEPS and resilience. I developed a daily gratitude practice, created affirmations, meditated, and journaled. I studied to understand and make peace with my thoughts and emotions. I became my own project and tested alternative healing methods like acupuncture, Reiki, emotional freedom technique (EFT, also known as "tapping"), past-life regression, hypnosis, and exercises from the HeartMath Institute. I rode other people's quiet horses to regain confidence and worked with horse trainers to strengthen my technique. I deepened my spiritual practice, took animal communication classes, and paid closer attention to nature's wisdom. I began to feel whole.

In 2009, a new life emerged. It started with a beautiful white racing pigeon we called Paloma Blanca. She flew into our lives in the spring and stayed for six weeks. She became my constant companion. She marched with me down the barn aisle as I fed the horses. She muttered little comments as we walked about the barn. She roosted above the stalls at night. She made me laugh. Her presence seemed to bring lightness, healing, and joy to all.

New initiatives took flight. I began writing articles for the local paper to help people affected by the recession. This pushed me to start the company that I had been pondering and to develop business cards. A boarder's horse recovered from serious colic, traveled to a national competition, and received the highest dressage award of his career. Another boarder's horse made visible progress in her recovery from a hard-to-diagnose metabolic disorder. The horses gleamed with good health. We gave a nod to Paloma for this good fortune.

One late afternoon, I sat in the grass to relax and watch Paloma eat her dinner. She picked up the grains with intensity, speed, and accuracy. As she ate, her head bobbed and her eye scanned the sky for predators. We saw a flock of chattering black birds flying toward us. Paloma stretched up tall, stared at the birds and flew off over the barn. Flying high above the treeline, she raced through the air, tracing the perimeter of our property. She streaked over the indoor arena, bent her wings and fell into a dive. Just before hitting the ground, she swooped up and rocketed back up in the air, circling our farm. It was shocking how she identified her "territory" so consistently with our property line. At almost dusk, her small white body shined against the blue sky as she jetted through the air. It was a most spectacular aerial display and quite intimidating. The black birds changed course. After watching them fly off, she swooped down and flew through the barn to her favorite perch. I walked into the barn and gazed up at her. She was all puffed up. I said, "Paloma Blanca, that was awesome!" There was no mistaking her pride.

She visited us twice more over the years. The last time was in 2016. What a gift she was to us all.

Later that same year, I found coaching. Actually it found me. Someone sent me an email about a weeklong program on executive coaching. I had never heard of executive coaching, but it sounded interesting. I took the course. It changed my life. The possibilities were infinite. I had reinvented into a stronger version of myself. What a gift.

Ten years later, I am writing this book and living by my own design. Without resilience strategies, I'm not sure where I would have ended up. My resilience practices sustain me, fuel me, and fill me with positivity, light, and clarity. They empower me to move forward and to notice the good no matter what the circumstances. I've built a business of my dreams and live surrounded by all that I love, including sweet Lemon Squeezy, another gift. Of course, there are still the challenges of being human and navigating a somewhat frenetic world, but life is good. I am so grateful.

Here are a few summary points on resilience. Most of all, use them to create a life you enjoy. The world needs your greatness.

Summary Points

1. Select your favorite resilience activities.

2. Schedule them on your calendar.

3. Do them!

4. Release judgment on whether they are working or if you're doing them "right."

5. Show up for yourself.

6. Suspend disbelief.

7. Live your greatness!

Conclusion

Congratulations! You've made it through the reinvention journey so far. We've covered a lot of ground together since we began.

We learned the five-step reinvention process and the states of transformation, what it takes to trust yourself and others, and how to follow the love and make great decisions. I shared the high-impact leadership model and the importance of positive fuel, clarity of vision, and how to take high-impact action. We suffered through my identity crises and learned tips to smooth out a bumpy transition. Lemon Squeezy helped us discover the power of the opposite and the value of boundaries and rules of engagement. We learned to break things down to see the truth of a situation and find our way forward to a breakthrough.

As we traveled this journey, I shared some of my favorite growth strategies, like how to lighten your load and the power of baby steps. We finished up with the MEPS, your resilience plan, and the inspiring Paloma Blanca, my angel bird.

Lemon Squeezy learned new ways to carry a human, his new physical "load." He challenged me to release old patterns, assumptions, and fears and open myself to new possibilities. I never thought I would retrain an ex-racehorse again. I thought I was too old, too damaged from old injuries, and not good enough. We worked together to release those fears and move forward with freedom, balance, and joy. It's an ongoing process.

Writing this book was part of the divine agreement I accepted the day I met Lemon Squeezy. I knew that his role was bigger than only being my riding horse. His calling was to teach, inspire, and show others what's possible, including me. He's done a magnificent job, and I am honored to be on this path with him. Our partnership has taken us both to new heights, and new opportunities continue to unfold.

Lemon Squeezy is becoming a masterful facilitator and he is well-loved by clients. He will continue to lead our Reinventing Greatness retreats. He and the herd will also continue to teach and inspire business professionals in our Alpha Horse Leadership workshops and speaking events. One of his new endeavors is to serve as an ambassador for The Thoroughbred Retirement Foundation and help support his fellow retired racehorses. He's following the love.

Our riding work together continues to build on a foundation of trust. He's smart, willing, and easy to ride when he feels safe and I am clear. He loves to work, and we've had many beautiful moments. In fact, some of the time it's "easy peasy." Perfect, eh? He also loves water. Our plans include trail riding, learning to swim, dressage, and I'll introduce him to jumping. We'll explore and see what he likes. Being able to choose what you want to do is one of the best parts of living by your own design.

Reinvention is an ongoing process of discovery. There are always new questions, new answers, better methods, and unexplored territory. There is no end. Growth is timeless. Learning is lifelong. New awareness starts a new process and sparks new insights. A new trail unfolds and invites you forward. It tempts and beckons. What will you do?

At any moment, you can choose to reinvent. Maybe it's just a small tweak. Maybe it's time for a full-scale overhaul. The choice is ever present. Your future is in your hands. You design your own experience.

As I look around, I am excited for the future. New seeds are being planted, new sprouts are emerging. I'm blessed to work with amazing people and organizations doing great work. I've known many of my clients for years and watched as they claimed their greatness, reinvented, and positioned themselves for deeper impact over and over again. They are thought leaders and entrepreneurs committed to excellence and to sharing their best with the world. It's a privilege to support them as they achieve their goals.

My path is clear. I say yes to more growth, yes to deepening and expanding connections, yes to living in harmony with our beautiful earth, and yes to thriving and doing what I love.

What will you say yes to?

Allow yourself to be open to the infinite possibilities.

The world needs your greatness. We need YOU.

Don't let fear steal your dreams. Challenge your assumptions. Be a safe place for yourself and others. Take high-impact action. Carry your load, and offload the rest. Follow the love. Savor small wins and give yourself treats. And be sure to rest and nourish yourself along the way.

What baby step will you take today? Go for it. Lemon Squeezy and I are by your side.

I wish you the best of success as you walk forward into the new. Thank you for joining me on this journey.

Shari J Goodwin

For More Information

For more information and to receive your free "10 Steps to High-Impact Leadership," featuring photos with Lemon Squeezy, go to www.jaeger2.com and sign up for our newsletter.

Contact Shari for information on private coaching, strategic planning, customized group retreats and training, and speaking events. We have numerous programs available and would love to help you achieve your goals.

Also join us on social media:
Facebook: facebook.com/ShariJaegerGoodwin
YouTube: www.youtube.com/user/ShariJaegerGoodwin
LinkedIn: www.linkedin.com/sharijaegergoodwin
Twitter: twitter.com/ShariJGoodwin
Instagram: www.instagram.com/sharijgoodwin

Here's to living and working by your own design!

About the Author

Shari J Goodwin is an innovative business strategist, leadership coach, author, speaker, and horsewoman with over 25 years of experience, including starting four companies and serving as Director of Program Strategy for a global engineering firm. One of the start-ups, an information technology staffing and consulting firm, generated $2.1 million in its first year. As a former environmental scientist, she led the development of winning proposals valued at up to $65 million, and supported the Clean Water Act regulatory development process. Her engineering team provided technical support for a case heard by the US Supreme Court.

She owns Jaeger2 and helps business owners and leaders position themselves for optimum impact and quality of life. Author of the inspirational Amazon best seller, *Take the Reins! 7 Secrets to Inspired Leadership*, Shari holds a master's degree in biology, undergraduate degrees in zoology and English, and is certified in executive coaching and equine-assisted psychotherapy. She is the founder of *Alpha Horse Leadership Training for HUMANS*™, an equine-assisted learning program specializing in building emotional intelligence skills and awareness of nonverbal communication.

Shari was a founding member of the board for George Mason University's Women in Business Initiative, is a board member of the Women's Business Council for the Fauquier Chamber of Commerce, serves as a member of the advisory board for the Be the Change Foundation, and holds memberships in Women in Technology, the Equine Experiential Education Association, and the International Coach Federation. She and Lemon Squeezy support The Thoroughbred

Retirement Foundation. She and her husband live on a horse farm outside of Washington, DC, with five horses, two dogs, and three barn cats. For more information on her services, see www.jaeger2.com.

Notes

1   See https://www.youtube.com/user/ShariJaegerGoodwin.

2   See https://www.merriam-webster.com/dictionary/reinvention.

3   David Neagle, *The Art of Success II* (audio CD), 2012. David is also the author of *The Millions Within: How to Manifest Exactly What You Want and Have an EPIC Life!* (Morgan James Publishing, 2013).

4   Rachel Conerly, "The Three Dimensions of Trust," Collaborative Leaders, Inc., 2012. Her firm, www.thecos.org, uses the model. It is not a book, but a worksheet they use in their trainings.

5   Adapted from Alexander Caillet, "The Thinking Path," chap. 18 in *On Becoming a Leadership Coach: A Holistic Approach to Coaching Excellence,* ed. Clarice Scriber, Christine Wahl, and Beth Bloomfield (New York: Palgrave Macmillan, 2008), 149–166.

6   https://www.heartmath.com/blog/ why-is-the-heart-brain-connection-so-important/.

7   https://www.heartmath.org/research/science-of-the-heart/ energetic-communication/.

8   https://www.hopkinsmedicine.org/health/healthy_aging/
    healthy_body/the-brain-gut-connection.

9   https://www.mountsinai.org/about/newsroom/2018/your-gut-is-
    directly-connected-to-your-brain-by-a-newly-discovered-neuron-
    circuit-emily-underwood.

10 Their website is www.polaritypartnerships.com.

11 See www.gallupstrengthscenter.com.

12 I often refer to her book *You Can Heal Your Life* (Hay House,
    1984), among others.

13 https://www.gallup.com/workplace/236561/employees-strengths-
    outperform-don.aspx.

14 Wong Kiew Kit, *The Complete Book of Chinese Medicine* (Cosmos
    Internet, 2002).

Made in the USA
Middletown, DE
03 June 2019